EXPLAIN THE CLOUD LIKE I'M 10

LEARN THE INNER-SECRETS BEHIND KINDLE,
NETFLIX, AWS, APPLE, FACEBOOK, AND
GOOGLE.

TODD HOFF

POSSIBILITY OUTPOST INC.

CONTENTS

About the Author   v

1. Starting Our Journey   1
2. What Does the Cloud Look Like?   4
3. Why is it called a 'cloud' anyway?   12
4. If You Use Online Banking You Already   21
   Understand The Cloud
5. What is the Cloud?   29
6. What is a Service?   33
7. What is a Cloud Service?   38
8. Facebook Messenger is a Cloud Service. How does   42
   it Work?
9. What isn't a Cloud Service?   50
10. What does Stuff Mean?   59
11. What does Stored in the Cloud Mean?   64
12. What is a Device?   69
13. What is a Program or App?   72
14. What is the Internet?   77
15. What is a Datacenter?   86
16. What is Cloud Computing?   91
17. The Good, the Bad and the Ugly of Cloud   146
    Services
18. Kindle: Amazon's Cloud Service for Reading   158
    Ebooks
19. iCloud: Apple's Cloud Service for Syncing Data 167
20. Google Maps: A Cloud Service for Navigation   174
21. Cloud DVR: TV in the Cloud   182
22. Netflix: What Happens When You Press Play?   187

23. Fighting the Ecosystem Wars in the Proactive Cloud   235

24. Does stormy weather affect cloud computing?   258

25. If I say Something is in the cloud, do you know what it means?   261

26. We've Come to the End of our Journey   272

What readers are saying...   275

Also by Todd Hoff   281

ABOUT THE AUTHOR

Why should anyone believe a book on the cloud, written by me, is worth reading?

Let me make my case. That's what a bio is for, right?

I've been a programmer for more than 30 years. Yes, 30 years. I know, it's hard to believe. It's hard for me to believe, that's for sure!

I graduated from the University of Oregon with a Bachelor of Science, Computer Science and a Bachelor of Science, Business Administration, Decision Science.

I was a decent student, but I turned out to be a good programmer. Like any job, being a programmer has its ups and downs, but I'd highly recommend it as a career. I've been a dishwasher, janitor, waterbed installer, and I even carried logs around for a while at a mill. Programming is much easier than any of those jobs.

I've worked in Silicon Valley my entire career, so I've been able to work at companies like NEC, System Industries, IBM, Convergent, Litton Integrated Automation, Sun Microsystems, PAC Bell, Silicon Graphics, Intuit, Hitachi, and Yahoo, to name just a few.

I was lucky enough to be involved in a successful optical switch startup, Lightera, that was sold to Ciena Corporation.

I've taught database courses at UCSC and Perl programming for Sun. I enjoyed teaching a lot.

For the last decade, I've run a blog called HighScalability, which has covered the cloud space in detail since the very beginning. I was a very early user of AWS, and I've been using it ever since. So I think I have a pretty good idea of how the cloud works at both a theoretical and practical level.

As for writing, I've written hundreds of articles for my blog. Most of the articles are something like this book, although written for a more technical audience. I try to clearly explain complex topics. So that's what probably gave me the hubris to think I could write this book.

This is not my first book. Over the years, I've written several books. I don't think I'm a great writer, but I think I write well enough to get my point across, and that's the most important skill when writing a book like *Explain the Cloud Like I'm 10*.

Does all this make me qualified to write a beginning book on the cloud? I honestly don't know. I have a feeling nobody is really qualified enough, but I thought a book like this was necessary, so I took my best shot at it.

You can see my resume here if you're interested.

https://www.facebook.com/Todd-Hoff-424067847964902/
https://www.amazon.com/Todd-Hoff/e/B071SKC31T
toddhoffious@gmail.com

1

STARTING OUR JOURNEY

Do you have cloud induced FOMO (fear of missing out)?

Here's the definition of FOMO: *anxiety that an exciting or interesting event may currently be happening elsewhere, often aroused by posts seen on a social media website.*

Is that you? When you hear about the cloud, do you get a little anxious because you don't know what the cloud is? Do you feel like technology is passing you by? Do you feel like the future is leaving you behind and you'll never catch up?

If you do...no wonder! We hear about the cloud all the time these days. And I mean all the time. Every day there's a new cloud-based dating app; a new cloud-based gizmo for your house; a new cloud-based game; or a thousand other new things—all in the cloud.

The cloud is everywhere! Everything is in the cloud! What does it mean!

Let's slow down. Take a deep breath. That's good. Take another. Excellent. This book is how you overcome Cloud FOMO.

I'll let you in on a little secret: **the cloud is not that hard to understand**. It's not. It's just that nobody has taken the time to explain to you what the cloud is. They haven't, have they?

Deep down I think this is because they don't understand the cloud either, but I do. I've been a programmer and writer for over 30 years. I've been in cloud computing since the very start, and I'm here to help you on your journey to understand the cloud. Consider me your tour guide. I'll be with you every step of the way, but not in a creepy way.

I take my time with this book. I go slow and easy, so you can build up an intuition about what the cloud really is, one idea at a time.

When you finish reading, you'll understand the cloud. When you hear someone say some new cool thing *is in the cloud,* you'll understand exactly what they mean. That's a promise.

How do I deliver on that promise? I use lots and lots of pictures. I use lots and lots of examples. We'll dive into the secret inner-workings of Amazon Web Services (AWS), Netflix, Facebook Messenger, Amazon Kindle, Apple iCloud, Google Maps, Nest and cloud DVRs.

You'll learn by seeing and understanding; no matter if you're a complete beginner, someone who knows a little and wants to learn more, or a programmer looking to change their career to the cloud.

I'm excited. This will be fun. Let's get started!

2

WHAT DOES THE CLOUD LOOK LIKE?

Everyone talks about the cloud like it's some vague, abstract thing, when in fact it's a real material thing you can see and touch.

So before we get into the nitty gritty of defining what the *cloud* is, let's make the cloud real by taking a peek at what it looks like:

Facebook

That's a strange image, isn't it? How is this a picture of the cloud everyone talks so much about?

What you're looking at is the interior of a *datacenter* owned by Facebook. A datacenter is just a giant warehouse-sized building containing lots and lots of computers and other equipment.

How many computers? See those big glowy things in the picture? Each big glowy thing is called a *rack* and is about the size of a side-by-side refrigerator.

Notice how racks line both sides of the hallway, as far as the eye can see? Row after row of such hallways fill a datacenter.

If you do the math, the number of computers in a datacenter

can range from tens of thousands to hundreds of thousands. That's a lot of computers!

Let's look a little closer.

Here's what one of the racks looks like:

Facebook

Each rack holds dozens of pizza-box sized computers that look like:

Open Compute

You've probably never seen a computer like this before. It's specially built to fit in a rack and racks are specially built to fit in datacenters.

Computers slide into a rack like a drawer slides into a cabinet:

Facebook

Nothing magical going on here. Racks are simply a way of stuffing as many computers together as humanly possible.

Now I can tell you a secret. The cloud is just a **big building with a lot of computers** inside. That's all the cloud is. Lots and lots of computers. Not such a big deal, is it?

So far we've only seen a Facebook datacenter, but a datacenter from Google, Amazon, or Microsoft will look similar.

The inside of a Google datacenter looks like:

Google

All those pipes are part of a cooling system for keeping Google's computers happy and healthy.

An Amazon datacenter looks a lot like a Facebook datacenter:

Amazon

We've seen what datacenters look like on the inside; let's take a gander at the outside.

Here's the outside of a Facebook datacenter:

Facebook

And here's the outside of a Microsoft datacenter:

Microsoft

Not that different than a Costco or Walmart, are they? But instead of selling quality brand-name merchandise, the cloud sells *computers as a service*. All that means is you can rent computers over the internet. We'll talk a lot more about selling *computers as a service* later.

When the cloud seems abstract and hard to understand, I want you to think back to these pictures.

At the simplest level, a cloud is just a big building full of computers. That's all it is. Nothing special is going on. There's no reason to feel intimidated.

See, you already know what the cloud is, and we just got started!

Now let's learn how *the cloud* got its name.

3

WHY IS IT CALLED A 'CLOUD' ANYWAY?

It's thought the term *cloud* comes from the symbol used to represent a network when drawing flowcharts and diagrams.

Why is it called a *cloud* in the first place? *Cloud* is such a strange name. It's one of those annoying words that doesn't give you any hint about what it means.

How can a building full of computers be anything like the fluffy clouds we see in the sky?

The term *cloud* has a very practical origin. When engineers build stuff, they first draw a diagram of what they want to build.

On those diagrams, they use *symbols* to represent the different things they are building.

When building a house, for example, you use a symbol for a door instead of drawing a detailed picture of the exact door you want, knowing details like that will be figured out later (probably after quite a few arguments).

Wikimedia Commons

Let's say you are an engineer and you want to draw the

diagram of a computer network that would end up looking something like this:

You can see all the computers connected by wires, all the tables, all the people; it's a mess! Would you really want to draw something like that? No way. No more than you would draw all the doors in a house plan. You would create a symbol to represent a network.

And that's exactly what the engineers did. The symbol engineers chose to represent a network was that of a *cloud.*

A cloud symbol on a diagram will always look something like:

Why a cloud?

Nobody knows for sure, but it's actually a brilliant choice.

Clouds are easy to draw. Clouds can be any size. So can networks. Clouds can have almost any shape. So can networks. We only see the outside of a cloud; what happens on the inside is hidden from view. We don't care how a network works. Clouds are made up of gazillions of tiny drops of water or ice crystals. Networks of made up of many pieces of equipment.

So it makes sense to represent a network as a cloud. They have a lot in common.

Using the cloud symbol, our new diagram looks a lot cleaner:

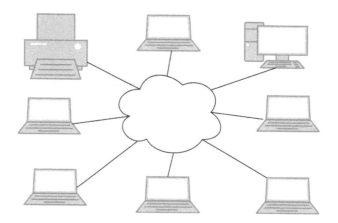

Local Area Network

It's simple and gets the point across, without all the messy real world details. Exactly what we want in a diagram.

The cloud symbol can represent *any network*; it doesn't matter what the network looks like or how it works.

What's a network?

A network connects things together.

A WiFi network connects computers to the internet. A highway system is a network of roads connecting places together. A cellular network is a network of equipment connecting phones together. A social network is a network connecting people together. A television network is a network of TV stations for showing program content. The IP Backbone Network is a network connecting all the devices that make up the internet.

These are all examples of networks. They are all very different in how they work and how they are built. Yet, we use the cloud symbol to represent all of them.

'The cloud' is short for cloud computing.

Remember our datacenter full of computers? It's just another network. All those computers connected together are made accessible over another network, the internet.

It was just a short jump from there to invent the term *cloud computing*. The term *cloud computing* was coined to mean accessing computer services over the internet.

That kind of makes sense, right?

In time, as cloud computing became a big business, cloud computing was shortened to just *the cloud*.

Whenever you hear *the cloud* now, it doesn't mean any network, it means a network of computers, accessed over the internet, that provides some sort of service. You don't care where those computers are located or how they work. You never see them. You never touch them. They are just a cloud of networked computers for you to use.

Let's Look at an Example Cloud Diagram

To see how the cloud symbol is used in real-life, here's a diagram of a complicated network:

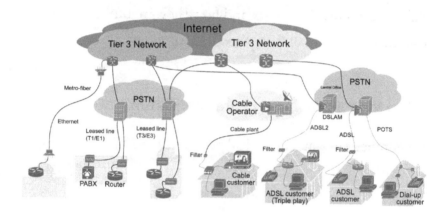

Wikimedia Commons

This diagram shows how various parts of the internet connect together. In fact, this is how your home network connects to others on the internet.

Don't worry; it doesn't matter if you understand the whole diagram. Focus on the parts that look like clouds.

You should be able to see a bunch of different cloud symbols. There are two PSTN (public switched telephone network) clouds. There's a Cable Operator cloud. There are two Tier 3 Network clouds. A Tier 3 Network connects your home to the internet (think Comcast and Verizon). And there's one big internet cloud at the top connecting everything together.

This diagram is old. Since a lot of people connect to the internet these days using their cell phone, if it were drawn today, it would include a cloud for cellular networks.

Let's just look at one cloud, the PSTN. If you don't remember, ancient land line phones look something like:

A complete diagram of the PSTN would contain a huge number of phones, an uncountable number of telephone poles, miles of cable, and an immense amount of electronic switching equipment.

It would be impossible to draw such a thing. Instead, we just draw a cloud symbol to represent the whole thing. We don't even bother trying to draw all the parts.

We don't care how many phones or telephone poles are in the PSTN. All we care about is we dial a number, and we can talk to anyone in the world. How it works doesn't matter.

Same for the other networks in the diagram. The internet is hugely complicated. Don't care. All we care about is that we can connect to any other computer in the world over the internet.

Isn't that cloud symbol handy?

So now you know how that annoying phrase—*the cloud*—came to be.

Interested in more details? You might like Who Coined 'Cloud Computing'?

4

IF YOU USE ONLINE BANKING YOU ALREADY UNDERSTAND THE CLOUD

Now that we've developed an intuition for what the cloud looks like and where the name came from, let's try to develop an intuitive feel for how the cloud works.

You've probably been using a cloud service for years; you've just never realized it. What is it? Your bank!

Banking has changed a great deal over recent years. To see how much, let me ask you a few questions.

How often do you go to the bank these days? Probably not as much as you used to. Standing in line to see the teller isn't much fun.

How often do you write a check anymore? Again, probably not as much as you used to. Paying bills online is so easy.

Do you know your bank teller's name? Probably not.

Do you carry a lot of cash with you? Why when credit/debit cards are so convenient?

If you think banking has changed for you, imagine a time traveler from the 19th century, they wouldn't even recognize banking today. In their era a bank in a small town might look something like:

In those days depositing money in the bank literally meant placing your money in a small iron safe. Bank robbers loved those safes. They cracked like a thin shelled egg.

Remember all those old Wild West movies where bank robbers dramatically rode away with the town's money?

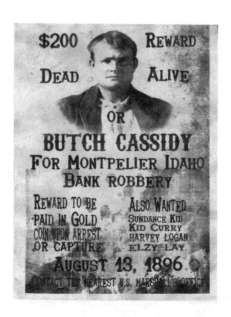

by Randy Franks

On the movie screen, Butch Cassidy robbing a bank is exciting, even romantic. In reality, that's your hard earned cash they're stealing. As a kid I remember laughing as the townsfolk rustled up a posse, thinking there's no way a backwater sheriff along with a bunch of bankers, butchers, and bakers would ever catch our "heroes." As an adult, I now understand their urgency. Your life savings hung in the balance. If the outlaws make a clean get away, you're instantly penniless. Who wouldn't ride hard for justice?

Today, bank robberies don't scare depositors at all. Why? Technology has totally transformed both the nature of money and banking.

Money is Just a Number in a Computer

If Butch Cassidy were alive today, he wouldn't be a bank robber; he'd be a hacker because that's where the money is. Money today is just a number stored in a computer. And that changes everything.

Do you go into a bank anymore to check your bank balance? Of course not, that's so old school. Now you check your balance at an ATM, using an app on your phone, or from a website.

When checking your bank balance using an ATM, do you think a team of bank tellers runs back into the vault to count your fat stacks of cash?

Of course not. Nobody thinks that. Everyone knows their bank balance is just a number in a computer. The days of small iron safes are long gone. We intuitively know the computer always knows our bank balance and displaying it is as simple as asking a computer.

What else has changed? Think about what happens when paying for dinner with a debit card. You swipe your card. Swiping subtracts money from your bank account and adds it to the restaurant's account.

On the swipe of your card does our ready team of bank tellers rush into the vault and snatch stacks of cash off your pile and toss them onto the restaurant's cash pile?

Of course not. Numbers update in a computer. That's all that's happening. The number representing your bank balance decreases and the number representing the restaurant's bank account increases by the same amount.

Where does all this occur? Good question, I'm glad you asked. All the numbers are stored and **updated in the bank's cloud**. You knew we had to get back to the cloud eventually.

Remember what the cloud looks like? It's a big building full of computers. Your bank built a cloud, with lots and lots of computers. That's where your money is stored, as numbers, on their computers, in their cloud.

Checking Balances on an ATM — How does it Work?

You're at an ATM; you enter a valid PIN code. You press the "show me my bank balance" button. What happens next?

The ATM talks to the bank's cloud over an electronic communication network, which is a lot like the phone system, only it doesn't transmit your voice; it transmits your data.

When the ATM talks to the cloud, it requests your balance. That request is routed to one of the computers in the bank's cloud. The computer knows who you are because you inserted a card identifying yourself. The computer looks up your balance and returns it back to the ATM.

What language do computers use to talk?

It's not so very different from words written in a letter. In fact, the whole process resembles an exchange of letters; only it's blisteringly fast because the exchange happens electronically.

The ATM sends a letter to the cloud, the cloud replies with a letter. Many letters are exchanged. Some letters are filled with requests; some are filled with information. A request looks like "send the bank balance for Joe." And an informational reply contains a number like Joe's bank account balance.

That back and forth style of exchange is how work gets done. Humans work the same way. We talk to each other. We ask each other questions. We ask each other to do things. Eventually, a task gets completed.

Of course, computers don't actually exchange letters. They exchange electronically transmitted packets of data, but the idea is the same.

Paying With a Debit Card — How does it Work?

The same process occurs when you pay for a meal with a debit card at a restaurant. You swipe your card on the card reader. The card reader talks to the cloud, letting it know who you are, which restaurant you're in, and how much the meal cost. A computer in the bank's cloud takes money out of your account and adds it to the restaurant's account. You're now free to leave the building.

What I just described, checking a bank balance and paying with a debit card, are services the bank provides. The bank implements both services using their *cloud,* so when you pay with a debit card or check your balance, those tasks are accomplished using a *cloud service.*

That's what a cloud service is, it's the things you can make a computer do for you.

If you're ever unclear about how the cloud and cloud services work, think back to this example. All these years when you've been using your bank, you've been using—unbeknownst to you—both a cloud and a cloud service.

So don't worry, you got this!

5

WHAT IS THE CLOUD?

A cloud is just a bunch of a computers in a datacenter.

That's the short definition. Here's my more complete definition of the cloud. You won't find it described like this anywhere else, but I think it will help make the cloud easier to understand:

The *cloud* is a *real physical place*—accessed over *the internet*—where a *service* is performed for you or where your *stuff* is *stored*. Your *stuff* is stored in the cloud, not on your device because the cloud is not on any device; the cloud lives in *datacenters*. A *program* running on your device accesses the cloud over the *internet*. The cloud is *infinite, accessible from anywhere*, at *any time*.

I'm going to explain each italicized word in the above paragraph. I'll keep on explaining things until I get to a point where I don't think more explanation will help you understand any better. The idea is you can keep reading and rereading explanations until it all makes sense in your head.

Along with explanations, I'm going to use lots of examples. I'm going to explain in some detail how several real cloud services work. I'll also explain how services that aren't cloud-based work. Comparing the two approaches will reveal a lot about the cloud.

By explaining all the key terms and showing what they mean through examples, I hope the clouds will part, and all will become clear. That's the idea anyway.

Let's start by defining *real physical place*. This is easy. We already did it! In the chapter, *What Does the Cloud Look Like?*, we showed how a cloud is a bunch of computers that live in a gigantic building called a datacenter.

The cloud is real; it's physical, you can reach out and touch it;

it even has a postal address. So the cloud is nothing to be afraid of.

If you do have a hard time understanding all these new concepts and ideas, don't worry, it's not you. This stuff is weird and hard to understand. It's so abstract. It deals with all sorts of intangible things like programs, data, services, and the internet.

I'll explain ideas in multiple ways, at times it may even seem like I'm repeating myself. At times it may even seem like I'm repeating myself, but I'm betting one of those approaches will help you make sense of things.

There are Really Two Kinds of Clouds: Cloud Providers and Cloud Services

There are really two kinds of clouds: *Cloud Providers* and *Cloud Services*. This gets confusing because in the news both will be called *the cloud* when they're two different things.

You will almost always use *cloud services*. Those are services running on a cloud. Remember how your bank offered services on their cloud? Apple's iCloud is a cloud service for keeping all your iOS devices in sync. It runs on Apple's cloud. Facebook Messenger is a cloud service for sending messages. It runs on Facebook's cloud.

As a programmer, I use *cloud providers*. Cloud providers own those datacenters we talked about earlier. Cloud providers let customers rent their computers to build services, just like you would go down to the local tool shed and rent a cement mixer, only the computers stay in the datacenter. They don't come home with you.

A cloud provider you may have heard of is Amazon Web Services (AWS). AWS is used by thousands of different companies to help deliver their services. You may have heard of some of them: Airbnb, BMW, Capital One, GE, Netflix, Intuit, Johnson & Johnson, NASA, Nordstrom, and Yelp.

To more deeply understand the difference between the two kinds of clouds, we'll need to talk about what a *service* is.

6

WHAT IS A SERVICE?

A service is a job you hire someone to do for you.

The meaning of the word *service* seems obvious until you try to define it. Since we'll be using the word *service* a lot, it's important we have a good feel for what it means.

A service is **a job you hire someone to do for you**. You could hire help because it's a task you can't do for yourself, you just don't want to do, or you simply don't have time to do.

It doesn't matter why. The key is you hire another party to do a job for you, so you don't have to do it yourself.

We Use Services all the Time

We hire services all the time in real-life. In fact, about 80% of the US economy revolves around services. Services are everywhere.

If you, for example, don't want to clean your house, you hire a house cleaning service. If you don't want to wash your car, you take it to a car wash. If you don't want to do your taxes, you use a tax professional. If you have kids, you hire a baby-sitter. If your car breaks down, you hire a mechanic. If you're planning a wedding, you hire a wedding planner, who will hire a venue, a caterer, a florist, a band, a photographer and dozens of other costly services.

All the services we just talked about are examples of concrete services. You get something you can see, touch, feel, or experience in exchange for money.

There are other types of services that are less tangible. If you buy a cell phone, you need network connectivity, so you hire a company like Verizon or AT&T to provide network service.

Electricity is another intangible service. Your house needs electricity so you hire the power company to deliver it to you.

The cloud is more like an intangible service. Water and power services are called utilities. In a way, a cloud provider creates a utility for computer services.

With that foundation, we can now understand the kind of services a cloud provider offers.

A Cloud Provider Rents Computers as a Service

A *cloud provider* is a company that owns a lot of computers and rents them out as a service. *Rent* means you pay good hard cash for using a cloud provider's computers.

Who are the major cloud providers?

The main cloud provider players today are Amazon AWS, Google Cloud Platform, and Microsoft Azure. There are many others, but these are the biggest and most popular.

For the most part, you don't have to care about cloud providers, no more than you care about who provides your electricity, water, or garbage service. You'll use a cloud service built on computers rented from a cloud provider; you will never have to deal with the cloud provider yourself.

What kind of services do cloud providers rent?

I'm going to list a lot of things that probably won't make sense to you, but here are some of the services a cloud provider can rent: compute, memory, storage, network bandwidth, caching, database, geographical diversity, disaster recovery, high availability, security, load balancing, authentication, search, machine learning, translation, image recognition, voice recognition, natural language parsing, DNS, payments, billing, queueing, notifications, email, and lots more.

Not every cloud provider offers all these services, but if you are a software developer, cloud services make your job a lot easier.

Why would anyone want to rent computers as a service?

For the same reason we use any service: we want all the benefits without all the work. All it costs is money!

The cloud provider is responsible for buying, maintaining, and operating their computers. All you have to do to use them is rent them. Everything else is taken care of for you. No muss, no fuss.

A Cloud Provider is Like a Car Rental Agency

Let's try a simple illustration. When you're traveling and you need a car, where do you go? A car rental agency. The car rental agency will always have cars for you to rent. That's the service a car rental agency provides. You don't own the cars. You don't have to buy the cars, store them, maintain them, repair them, or care about them at all. You rent a car when you need a car, and return it when done. That's **car rental as a service**.

A cloud provider is **computer rental as a service**. Just use a computer and return it when you're done. As with everything we're talking about, it's more complicated than that, but that's the basic idea.

7

WHAT IS A CLOUD SERVICE?

A cloud service performs a job for you in a cloud.

We now know what a service is and we know what a cloud provider is. When we put them together, we get a *cloud service*. Imagine that!

What kind of job does a cloud service perform?

There are more cloud services than you can shake a stick at. Probably the most common job people hire a cloud service to do for them is file sharing and storage. A service like Dropbox, for example, offers a way to backup your data in their cloud and sync it onto all your devices.

To get a feel for how many services there are, here's a list with a description of the job each service performs:

• **Facebook Messenger** - exchange messages with people you know on Facebook.

• **Amazon** - buy most everything; sell and distribute products through their fulfillment system.

• **Apple iMessage** - exchange messages with with people you know who have Apple devices.

• **YouTube** - watch videos.

• **Google Maps** - figure out where you are and how to navigate to other locations.

• **Amazon Kindle** - read ebooks.

• **Gmail** - send and receive email.

• **Instagram** - share filtered selfies.

• **Twitter** - tell strangers what you had for breakfast.

• **Salesforce** - manage the relationship with customers.

• **iCloud** - sync data between Apple devices.

• **Google Apps** - a suite of group productivity programs.

- **Google Translate** - translate text from one language to another.

- **Box** - securely, share and edit all your files from anywhere.

- **DocuSign** - digitally sign documents.

- **Google Photos** - store and manage photos.

- **Evernote** - take and manage notes.

- **Facebook** - get annoyed by people you barely know.

- **Mailchimp** - create and manage email lists.

- **QuickBooks** - online accounting.

- **Spotify** - listen to music.

- **Pandora** - listen to music.

- **Netflix** - watch videos.

- **Yelp** - rate and review business and services.

- **PayPal** - send money and pay bills.

- **Uber** - get a ride.

- **Square** - accept credit card payments from customers.

- **Amazon Drive** - store files.

- **Microsoft OneDrive** - store files.

• **Carbonite** - backup files.

• **Adobe Creative Cloud** - Photoshop, After Effects, and other high-quality image editors.

This is an abbreviated list. There are many, many more services out there.

Most new services these days are cloud services.

Why? The cloud has many advantages over programs that run on only one device. They are more reliable, more scalable, more powerful, and easier to program. We'll talk more about those advantages in chapters to come.

Right now, let's take a deeper look at cloud services by going in-depth on the inner-workings of *Facebook Messenger*.

8

FACEBOOK MESSENGER IS A CLOUD SERVICE. HOW DOES IT WORK?

What exactly does it mean when we say something is a cloud service?

It seems everyone is on Facebook these days, so let's use Facebook Messenger as our example of a cloud service.

If you're on Facebook you probably already know Facebook Messenger lets you send messages to other Facebook users.

Here's me sending a message using Messenger to Linda, my lovely wife and assistant for this trick, er, example:

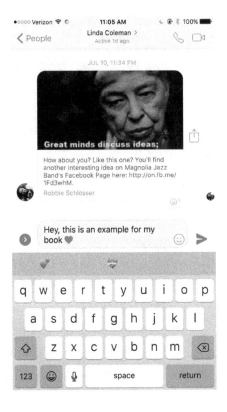

Even after all these years of using technology, it stills gives me a little thrill to know Linda received my message only a few seconds after I sent it, even though I was dozens of miles away when I pressed the send button. We take it for granted, but it's amazing.

On Linda's iPhone here's the message she received from me:

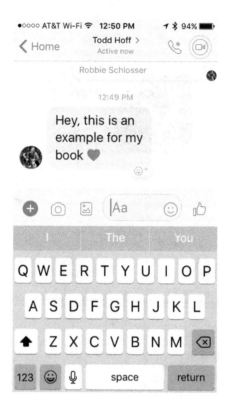

How did that message go from my phone to Linda's phone in the blink of an eye? You might have guessed the answer given the topic of this book: Facebook Messenger used the cloud to send my message to Linda.

A lot is going on here; let's unpack it.

First, we need to understand Facebook Messenger is a *program* or *app* that runs on a *device*. Let's quickly define each term. We'll go into more detail later.

A device is your smartphone, tablet, laptop, or desktop computer. It could even be a watch or a wearable. It could even be a gizmo in your house. It's any computer you happen to be using at the time.

The thing on the device that knows how to access the cloud is called an *app*. *App* is short for *application*. Facebook Messenger is an app. Tapping on the Facebook Messenger icon starts the app. You interact with the Messenger app to send and read messages.

Cloud services can also be accessed over the web, using a web browser like Chrome, Firefox, Internet Explorer, or Safari. In that case, you're using an app, the browser, to interact with a website over the internet. For our purposes, a website works like an app, so I'll treat websites and apps as the same throughout this book. Nothing changes.

In my example, the device I'm using is my iPhone. All my examples will use the iPhone, because, well, that's what I own. The app I'm using is Facebook Messenger. I downloaded Messenger, for free, over the internet, from Apple's App Store, on to my iPhone.

As you can see, the message I'm sending is "Hey, this is an example for my book." Great literature it's not.

When I tap the send button my message is sent to Linda. How? The cloud makes it happen.

Let's walk through how Messenger sends my message to Linda

- When I press send, the Messenger app takes my message, packages it up in an envelope, and sends it to Facebook's cloud over the internet, just like you would do when sending a letter. The package is called *data*. When you buy a data plan for your cellphone from Verizon or AT&T, this is the kind of data that counts against your data limit. There are separate chapters on both *data* and the *internet* later in the book.

- For now, you can think of data as both the letter and the envelope mailed using the postal service. You can think of the internet as a digital version of the highway the postal service uses to deliver letters. You can think of the name "Linda" as the address the letter is sent to. There's no stamp, so sending a message over Messenger doesn't cost you anything, which is why people like it so much!

- What does it mean to send my message to Facebook's cloud? It means my message is sent over the internet to one of the computers in one of Facebook's datacenters. Facebook has many datacenters around the world. Usually what happens is Messenger will pick the datacenter closest to you and send the message there.

- An app running on a computer in Facebook's datacenter reads the message, sees that I'm sending it to Linda, and puts the message in Linda's inbox. Facebook's inbox is just like the mailbox in which the postal carrier places your mail, except it's not physical, it's digital, it holds data, not letters.
- Linda also runs Messenger on her iPhone. The Messenger running on her phone (or any other device) will, over the internet, read her inbox in the cloud, see a new message is waiting, take it from the inbox, store it on her phone, and then display the message on her phone's screen for her to read. It's like you getting mail from the mailbox; only it happens using programs, data, and the internet instead of postal carriers, postal trucks, letters, and mailboxes.

So, that's what it means for a service to be performed in the cloud. Facebook's cloud was responsible for receiving the message, putting the message in the right inbox, and then handing over the message when requested. That's the basic service it performs. It may not sound like much, but in reality, the whole process is very complex. That's the idea though.

Once you develop an intuition for how Messenger sends

messages, you understand almost every cloud service out there. They all work in a similar way.

Two Points I'd Like You to Notice

The cloud is a separate place.

The cloud is a remote place. It's not on your phone. The cloud doesn't exist on any device you use; it runs on computers in a datacenter. You access the cloud through a program you install on your device. That program knows how to talk to the cloud over the internet. This is why you can use a cloud service on any device. It's the program, like Facebook Messenger, that gives you access to the cloud, and that program can potentially run on any device.

Your stuff is in the cloud, not on your phone.

The cloud is always there. It never sleeps. Your stuff is always available in the cloud. My messages to Linda are stored in Facebook's cloud.

Let's say Linda loses her phone (which has been known to happen). When she buys a new phone and installs Facebook Messenger, she will still be able to see all her old messages. That's because her messages were not stored on her old phone. They were stored in Facebook's cloud, and Facebook has a humongous inbox that never gets full.

Facebook is their Own Cloud Provider

In my story, did you notice Facebook owns their computers and their datacenters? Facebook doesn't use one of the cloud providers we mentioned earlier; Facebook is their own cloud provider.

Why would a company want to own a cloud?

The biggest reasons are **money** and **control**. When a company gets really big, like Facebook, it's far cheaper for them to own their own datacenters. Economies of scale apply.

The other advantage of running your own cloud is you have complete control. That control means you can tailor everything to give your users the best possible experience.

Netflix, a service for watching movies and TV shows over the internet, is an example of a company that doesn't own datacenters. Netflix uses AWS as their cloud provider. Why? They don't want to manage datacenters. It takes a lot of time, money, and effort to manage a bunch of datacenters. Netflix decided they didn't want the hassle; they just want to concentrate on building their service.

Both Netflix and Facebook are massively successful, so either approach works.

9

WHAT ISN'T A CLOUD SERVICE?

Any program that runs on only one computer can not be a cloud service.

I'll use my wife Linda in another example. I know she'll just love that. I can hear her kvetching at me now as she reads this sentence.

Linda is an accountant and EA (Enrolled Agent, which means she's a tax expert). In her job, she uses QuickBooks, which is a small business accounting software program from Intuit.

For the longest time, Intuit only made a desktop computer

version of QuickBooks. Now Intuit makes a cloud version called QuickBooks Online.

We're going to compare the two products as a way of understanding how big a difference there is between the two different approaches—cloud and desktop—of making and using software.

The Pain and Suffering of Using Desktop Computers

In case you haven't seen one in awhile, here's what an old desktop computer looks like:

Ah, the memories....

Software was sold in boxes!

How do you buy software for a desktop computer? It's quite the process.

First, you have to realize software used to come in boxes. Boxes? I know, right? How primitive.

If you haven't seen what a box of software looks like recently, here's a picture of a desktop version of QuickBooks:

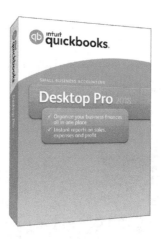

Linda uses a version of QuickBooks like this today, as do zillions of other accountants.

The desktop version of QuickBooks does have a nice looking interface. Here, take a look for yourself:

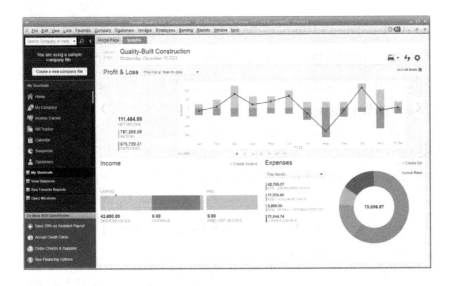

Nothing to complain about. It's state of the art. Buying boxed software is easy these days, but that wasn't always the case.

How did you buy box software in the olden days?

You had to drive across town to a retail store; browse shelves stuffed with awkward boxes of software packages; read the back matter on each box in a vain attempt to figure out what it does; finally pick a box off the shelf; take it to the checkout line and stand for ten minutes; pay with a check using your driver's license as ID; drive the box back to your office; install the software by inserting one floppy disk after another into a floppy drive, like an animal; pray it does what you want; scour the printed manuals to figure out how it works; wait on hold for hours as you call support to debug problem after problem.

As horrible as all this sounds, and it was horrible, at the time **it was awesome**. A program like QuickBooks made your job as an accountant a hundred times easier, but let's **look at the limitations**.

QuickBooks was installed on a single computer that had to be purchased, maintained, and upgraded. Only one person could use it at a time. You had to be sitting in front of the computer to use it. All your precious accounting data was stored on the hard drive of that one computer. If that computer died, all your data was lost. If you were across town and needed a report, you were out of luck; the computer was back in your office. If you bought a new computer, you had to repeat the whole installation process and move the accounting data from your old computer to your new computer. And every year upgrading to a new version required repeating the same install process.

There's a lot of power in desktop software, but there are also a lot of limitations. How can we fix them?

Becoming a Cloud Service Changes Everything

Intuit built a cloud version of QuickBooks to solve the problems we just talked about; it's called QuickBooks Online.

Here's what QuickBooks Online looks like. Look closely...

notice the difference between this version and the desktop version?

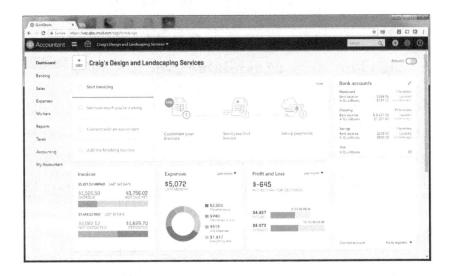

Did you notice the online version runs in the Chrome browser? At the top, you might be able to see the address bar containing Intuit's URL.

Yes, QuickBooks Online is a cloud service you use over the internet, as a website. That's what *online* means.

Many cloud services these days are websites instead of apps.

Why? Reduced development time and support costs.

Apps must be custom built for each type of device. The app for the Apple iPhone isn't the same as the app for an Android phone, so it takes a lot of time and money to write both.

In contrast, once you make a website, it will work from any web browser. That means any device with a web browser can use a service, and that's very attractive to software developers.

Let's look at the benefits of QuickBooks being an online cloud service available over the web.

To buy QuickBooks Online, you don't have to go to the store. Just point your web browser at the website and sign up. Registering only takes a few minutes. No checkout line! And you don't pay with a check; you pay over the internet with a credit card.

There's nothing to install. QuickBooks Online is already installed in Intuit's cloud. No floppy disks! This is a huge advantage for people who aren't handy with computers or small businesses without an IT department.

You can use QuickBooks Online from any computer, from anywhere in the world. You do not have to be in the office to use it. This is important. There are times on vacation when Linda receives an emergency call from a client. If her client uses QuickBooks Online, then Linda can help them from France, or anywhere we happen to be, as long as we have a good internet connection. There's not much she can do to help if her client uses the desktop version.

Another advantage of an online cloud service is many people can use it at the same time. You have to pay for each user of course, but the restriction of one person having to be in front of one particular computer in the office is gone.

What's also gone is the risk of data loss if your computer dies. QuickBooks Online keeps your data safe.

You also don't have to worry about upgrading your software anymore. Intuit controls the software running in their cloud. They're responsible for performing any and all upgrades. You probably won't even notice when an upgrade happens.

There's no software to install or upgrade. Get a new computer, just log in to the website like normal. You can use any computer you want, from anywhere in the world, any time you want.

There are other less obvious advantages of having Quick-Books as a cloud service. One key advantage is an external accountant can just log in and see how things are going with the business. That's not possible using desktop software.

It's not all wine and roses.

An advantage desktop applications usually have is they are more powerful, meaning they have more features and functions than the online versions of the same software. It's often easier for programmers to make sophisticated desktop software, programming a website requires more compromises. That's just something to consider.

You'll need to use the desktop version if it has a specific must have feature. Linda still uses the desktop version of Quick-Books for this very reason.

10

WHAT DOES STUFF MEAN?

To a computer, stuff is all just data.

Let's remember the first line from our definition of the cloud:

The *cloud* is a *real physical place*—accessed over *the internet*—where a *service* is performed for you, or where your *stuff* is *stored*.

So far we've talked about the cloud living in datacenters as a *real physical space*. What we need to talk about now is *stuff*. Your stuff.

You know what stuff is in your house. Look around. It's filled with stuff like pictures, furniture, those dirty clothes that never quite make it into the laundry hamper. Yes, I can see those from here.

Hopefully, you don't have rooms filled with this much stuff:

Wikimedia Commons

You have lots of stuff on your phone and other devices too. Here are some examples: photos of trips you've taken, music you listen to, movies you watch, email you ignore, text messages you send, calendar events you make, spreadsheets you create, and the documents you write.

The generic name for all these kinds of *stuff* is *data*. *Data* is a record of stuff. We refer to anything an app understands how to *do something with*—as data.

We've already seen an example of what *do something with* data means in the Facebook Messenger chapter. If you recall, the data in that scenario was the message I sent to Linda. Facebook Messenger is the app that knew how to take my message and send it to the cloud so it could be delivered to Linda.

One way to think of data is like **ingredients in a recipe**. Each ingredient is a piece of data. It's the chef, or in our case, a program, that knows how to whip the data up into a delicious meal.

On the iPhone, the camera app is the app you use to take a picture. The **camera app knows** how to *do something with* pictures. Take a picture and the camera app stores it on your phone as data. Later, if you look at the picture in your camera roll, the camera app knows how to read the data from your phone and turn it back into a picture. Send a picture to a friend, and it's the picture represented as data that is sent. An app on their phone (or other device) knows how to turn the data back into a picture again. Data and apps always work together like that.

If you're a Star Trek fan, do you remember how the transporter works? An object is converted into an energy pattern and stored in a pattern buffer. The pattern is then beamed to a location and reconverted into matter.

*Star Trek, sculpture by Devorah Sperber, Spock, Kirk
and McCoy: Beaming-In (In-Between), Microsoft,
Studio D, Redmond, Washington, USA*

The **pattern is data**. The transporter is the program that
knows what to do with the data. I hope, for Dr. McCoy's sake,
all the atoms are arranged in the right order!

Here's a less futuristic example of what *do something with
data* means. Let's say, as you receive receipts for purchases
you've made during the year, you toss them in a shoe box. At
the end of the year, your accountant asks for your receipts, so
you hand over the box. Your accountant cringes and gets to
work turning those receipts into tax deductions. How?

Printed on every receipt is a company name, address, date,
and dollar amount. Those are pieces of data, just like the
message was in our Messenger example. Your accountant
knows what to do with that data. Looking at the company
name, for example, your accountant follows a set of rules to

determine if a purchase is a business expense. That's the **accountant's job, knowing what to do with all the data** in your receipts.

Data can be used to represent any sort of stuff, like a movie, photo, a song, money, email, contracts, or even a hotel reservation. To a computer, stuff is all just data.

11

WHAT DOES STORED IN THE CLOUD MEAN?

Your stuff is stored on real, physical, pieces of equipment in a datacenter.

Let's take another look at the first line in our cloud definition:

The *cloud* is a *real physical place*—accessed over *the internet*—where a *service* is performed for you, or where your *stuff* is *stored*.

We talked about stuff, but we haven't talked about what *stored* means yet, let's do that now.

When you have too much stuff in your house, you rent a storage unit and move all your extra stuff into it; that's what *stored* means. Your stuff is now stored in a storage unit:

In our Facebook Messenger example, we talked about how all of Linda's messages are stored in the cloud, not on her phone. You can think of the messages as *stuff*, or as we know now —*data*. You can think of the cloud as the storage unit. When using a cloud service, all your data is stored in the cloud.

Remember how we made the cloud real by showing what computers in a datacenter look like? Let's do that for storage.

Here's what cloud storage looks like:

Backblaze Storage Vault (Backblaze)

What are we looking at here? A storage vault from a cloud backup service called Backblaze. Each refrigerator sized cabinet is crammed full of *hard disks*. A hard disk stores and provides fast access to large amounts of data.

Here's what a hard disk looks like:

A hard disk is like a packing box in which you put small little bits of this and that. In your rented storage unit, you pile those boxes on top of one another as a high as they'll go. The more boxes, the more you can store.

That's the same idea Backblaze applies to their storage vault. Backblaze packs as many hard disks as possible into each cabinet, which is why it can store so many petabytes of data.

How large is a petabyte? Huge! Enough to store over 4,000 photos every day of your entire life. A datacenter will have racks and racks of these, almost too many to count.

Here's what similar disk storage unit looks like in Facebook's datacenter:

Facebook

So, just like how the cloud runs in a datacenter, your stuff is stored on real, physical, pieces of equipment that are also in a datacenter.

When you think of storing your photos, music, videos, and all your other data in the cloud, you can think of it being stored in something like the storage units pictured above.

The details change, but every cloud provider stores data in a similar way. There's nothing special about any of this. I hope that helps demystify things.

12

WHAT IS A DEVICE?

A device is your smartphone, tablet, laptop, or desktop computer. These are just computers in different forms so we'll use device and computer interchangeably.

A device could be owned by you, or it could be supplied by your work, or maybe you're borrowing a device. A device is simply some form of computer you're using at any given time.

Devices come in many forms: iPhone, iPad, Android Tablet, Android Smartphone, Microsoft Surface, Dell Inspiron, Acer Aspire, or Google Chromebook.

They may all appear different, but for our purpose, they all work pretty much the same. They run an app that accesses the cloud over the internet. How they make that happen doesn't matter to us.

Let's use our Facebook Messenger example again. Imagine you wake up in the morning and use the Facebook Messenger app installed on your iPad to check if someone posted anything interesting during the night. Probably not, but it can happen. So, that's your first device of the day.

As you're sipping your morning beverage of choice, your phone chirps with an alert. A friend sent you a not very funny joke on Messenger, but their jokes are never very funny. That's your second device.

You get to work; your desktop computer has Messenger installed too. That's device number three.

Let's say you pick up an Android tablet or Google Chrome-book at work and log into Facebook Messenger to check to see if you have any messages. Those are devices four and five.

During the day you could ping-pong back and forth between different devices but two things remain constant: Messenger and the cloud.

You're using the Messenger app (or web interface) on all your devices. And on every device, Messenger accesses the cloud to process and store your messages.

The key point is: it doesn't matter what device you're using as long as it has an *app* running on it that knows how to access the cloud.

13

WHAT IS A PROGRAM OR APP?

The thing on a computer that knows how to access the cloud is called a *program* or *app*.

App is short for *application,* and an application is the same thing as a program. It's important to know both words—*app* and *program*—because they're interchangeable.

There many different examples of apps: Facebook Messenger, YouTube, Google Maps, Snapchat, Instagram, and Solitaire. Are you into games? If you play Candy Crush or Angry Birds, those are apps too.

On the iPhone, apps are downloaded from Apple's App

Store. On an Android device, apps are downloaded from Google Play.

What is an app?

An app is a *series of instructions* telling a computer what to do. Apps are what make our devices useful. Here's what the home screen of my iPad looks like:

Your phone, tablet, or laptop will likely look quite similar. It's full of apps! Each icon represents an app. Tapping any one of those icons starts the corresponding app. Starting an app causes the computer to read the app's program instructions, and the computer does whatever those instructions tell it to do. Tapping the Messenger icon, for example, starts Facebook

Messenger. Once Messenger starts, you can begin sending and receiving messages.

What do program instructions look like?

They're a lot like the instructions you follow when cooking a recipe. Instead of being called a recipe, program instructions are called *source code*.

Here's an example of what source code looks like:

```
77 exports.timestamp = function() {
78    var str = "";
80    var currentTime = new Date()
81    var hours = currentTime.getHours()
82    var minutes = currentTime.getMinutes()
84    if (minutes < 10) {
85       minutes = "0" + minutes
86    }
87    str += hours + ":" + minutes;
88    if(hours > 11){
89       str += "PM"
90    } else {
91       str += "AM"
92    }
94    return str;
96 }
```

It won't make a lot of sense unless you're a programmer, but let's try to understand what a program does in general. Understanding the code itself isn't important.

Imagine explaining to a friend something you know how to do well and they don't know how to do at all. Let's use starting a car as an example. Instructions to start a car might look something like:

- find the car key
- find the car
- open the door
- sit down in the seat
- make sure the car is in park
- insert the key in the ignition
- turn the key
- confirm the engine has started

Look at the picture of the source code again. Each line is an instruction to the computer, just like each line in the car starting instructions is an instruction to a human.

The thing about instructions is that they can always be broken down into a lot more instructions. Just the *find the car key* step could be a dozen instructions.

The act of creating instructions with enough detail that the person you're instructing will be able to start the car is called *programming*. The text of the written instructions is called a *program*. Whoever creates the instructions is a *programmer*. The thing that knows how to interpret the program is a *computer*.

Computers understand far simpler instructions than we used in our *Start the Car* example, but the idea is exactly the same.

Not long ago it was humans, mainly women, sitting at desks, who performed the calculations computers execute today:

Shorpy

If you're interested, Computing Power Used to Be Measured in 'Kilo-Girls', is a good read.

14

WHAT IS THE INTERNET?

The internet is an electronic highway system for sending data from one computer to another computer.

Let's take a look at our cloud definition once again:

The *cloud* is a *real physical place*—accessed over *the internet*—where a *service* is performed for you, or where your *stuff* is *stored*.

At the start of our journey, to make the cloud real, I showed you a picture of computers in a datacenter. Unfortunately, that won't be possible with the internet. The internet is real, it is physical, but the internet is so many different things connected together it's impossible to represent with a single picture.

So, let's start simply. The word *internet* is short for *interconnection of networks*. The easiest way to understand what *interconnection of networks* means is to think of the highway system.

Here's a picture of the interstate highway system in the US:

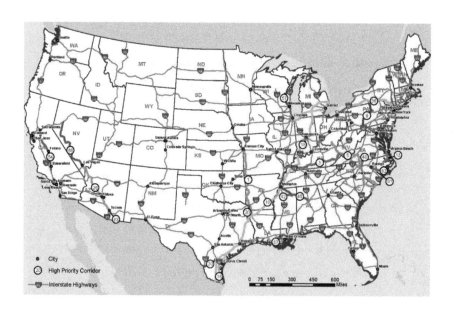

First, notice how the highway system is a network, where a

network is a *group or system of interconnected people or things*. In this case, the things in the network are highways.

A highway is a long stretch of concrete, over which cars and trucks can travel, in both directions, at high speeds.

Looking at the map, it's clear that all those highways connect together. You can exit off one highway and get on another. In other words, the highways *interconnect*. It's because highways interconnect that you can plan a route from one side of the country to the other. In fact, many routes will take you coast-to-coast.

That's all an *interconnected network* means: there's a system of paths such that you can plan a route from one place to another over the network.

OK, now let's consider the internet. You can think of the

internet as an electronic highway system for sending data from one computer to another computer. In other words, the internet allows computers to talk to each other.

The internet isn't made of concrete but from wires and cables strung across the globe. Electrical signals flow over all those wires and cables, carrying data from one place to another.

What does a map of the internet look like?

Opte Project 2015

Beautiful, isn't it?

The lines in the picture represent the wires and cables that form an interconnected network, just like the highway system.

Data, sent over the internet, follows a route across the network to get from your device to the cloud service, and then back again to your device, just like you are taking a cross-country trip in a car.

How do you get on the Internet?

Every highway has an onramp, a way for you to get on the highway. What is the onramp for the internet? For your devices, it will either be Wi-Fi or the cellular network. At home, if you have a cable service, it's likely your cable company providing your internet onramp.

When you stop at a coffee shop and search for a Wi-Fi connection, what you're doing is stringing your own *invisible wire* from your device to the internet. Wi-Fi isn't a physical wire, it's more like a radio signal, but the idea is the same, Wi-Fi is a way for data to flow from your device onto the internet.

The cellular network is just another way to string an invisible wire from your device to the internet. When you buy cellular service from Verizon, AT&T, or any other cell provider, your device talks to a cell tower, using something like a radio signal. It's the cell tower that connects you to the internet. Data flows from your device to the cell tower, to the internet, and back again over invisible wires.

Some of the Cables that Make Up the Internet

There are a few things I can show you that might make this desciption of the internet more concrete.

Here's an ethernet cable. A lot of internet traffic flows over cables that look like this:

ETHERNET

Port ←

Modular connector ←

Physical layer ←

Wikimedia Commons

Have you ever wondered how the internet gets from the US to Europe? Or from the US to Japan? Those are some big oceans to cross. You might be surprised to learn giant cables run along the ocean floor, carrying the internet from one continent to another.

Here's what one of those cables looks like:

Jan Messersmith (MadDog)

And here's a map of the many undersea cables carrying internet traffic across the world:

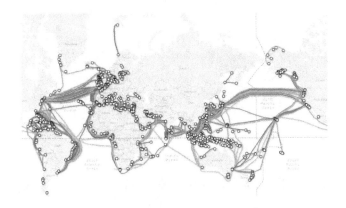

www.submarinecablemap.com

When I saw this map for the first time, I was shocked at how many under sea cables there were. Laying these cables must be immensely expensive. It seems people love their internet!

We talked about how your phone connects to the internet by first connecting to a cell tower. Here's what a cell tower looks like:

Wikimedia Commons

When your cell phone searches for a signal, it's looking for this kind of tower. Once connected, your data flows to the tower and then on to other parts of the network.

If you have a cable provider like Comcast, here's the type of cable connecting your house to the internet:

Tuan Nguyen

When you link all these kinds of cables together, along with many others kinds of cables and equipment, you create the internet.

15

WHAT IS A DATACENTER?

A datacenter is a giant warehouse-sized building containing lots and lots of computers and other equipment.

You were first introduced to the idea of a *datacenter* in chapter *What Does the Cloud Look Like?* I kept that chapter short and sweet because I didn't want to overwhelm you with information so early in the book. Here's, as they say, the rest of the story on datacenters.

What are datacenters for?

A datacenter is a building for housing computer systems and supporting components, such as networking and storage systems.

How many computers are in a datacenter?

It varies. A datacenter can have thousands, tens of thousands, or hundreds of thousands of computers.

Who builds datacenters?

Cloud providers. They build and own datacenters.

How much does a datacenter cost?

A lot. Modern datacenters can cost several billion dollars to build. Becoming a cloud provider requires deep pockets the size of the Marianas Trench, which is why there are so few of them.

Where are datacenters located?

Everywhere. A cloud provider can own one, a few, or dozens of datacenters located in every part of the world. The bigger a cloud provider is, the more datacenters they will have around the globe.

Why locate datacenters across the globe?

It's all about speed. The closer a datacenter is to users the faster computers in the datacenter can connect to users over the internet. That's why cloud providers build datacenters near large population centers. Faster internet connections make for a better user experience. Who likes to use a slow service?

A cloud provider like Google owns datacenters in around 17 different regions of the world. Accurate estimates are difficult to establish because Google is building new datacenters all the time, but this map should give you some idea of their vast geographical coverage:

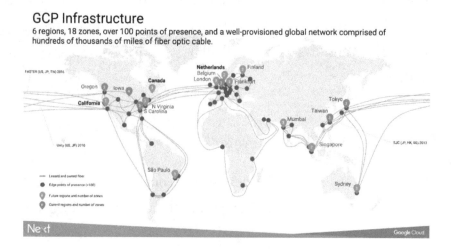

GCP Infrastructure
6 regions, 18 zones, over 100 points of presence, and a well-provisioned global network comprised of hundreds of thousands of miles of fiber optic cable.

Amazon also has datacenters all over the world:

As does Microsoft:

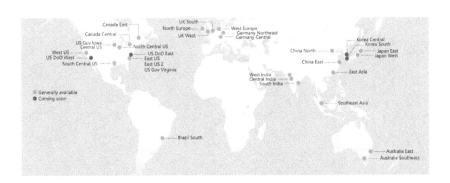

Wherever you are in the world one of their datacenters will be near you. That means faster service and faster is always better.

How many computers does a cloud provider have?

It's a secret. Really. They don't like to tell. Rumors suggest Google owns more than 2.5 million computers, but as I said, we don't know. What we do know is Google has oodles of computers, and they're buying more all the time.

16

WHAT IS CLOUD COMPUTING?

Cloud services run in *the cloud*. Cloud computing is just one of many services available in *the cloud*.

After *the cloud* the next most confusing phrase has to be *cloud computing*.

Cloud computing is big business these days and always seems to be in the news.

You might have read Amazon's cloud computing business has grown so much it's now more profitable than their online retail business.

Here's a quote from Reuters:

Amazon's revenue has soared in recent years as shopping has moved online and businesses have moved their computing operations to the cloud, where Amazon Web Services (AWS) is the biggest player. AWS accounts for a majority of Amazon's operating profit.

Microsoft also wants to move away from selling their Windows operating system to rely more on their Azure cloud computing platform. Google, with their Google Cloud Platform (GCP), wouldn't mind doing the same thing.

Cloud computing is the *new electricity* and everyone's fighting to be the new utility provider of choice.

We've had to wait to talk about cloud computing in detail because before we can make sense of it, we've first had to talk about *the cloud, cloud services, data, storage, the internet,* and *datacenters.*

Phew! That's a lot to understand. Now let's dive deeper.

Cloud and Cloud Computing are Used to Mean the Same Thing, but they Aren't

The most confusing thing about cloud computing is that words *the cloud* and *cloud computing* are used interchangeably when in fact they aren't the same thing.

Unfortunately, we just have to get used to that. To the uninitiated, *the cloud* and *cloud computing* can and do mean the same thing. No amount of scolding or finger-wagging will change that.

So most of the time when you hear *the cloud* or *cloud computing* you can mentally substitute one for the other and you'll do just fine.

But you didn't buy this book to learn what everyone else knows; you want to know the insider information.

Not everyone will agree with what I'm going to say next. It's a more nuanced view of the industry, but I think it will help you develop a deeper understanding of what's really going on.

The Cloud is Where Cloud Services Run, Cloud Computing is Just One Such Service

When you go to the website for Amazon Web Services (AWS), which is Amazon's cloud product (not their retail store), and look at all the cloud services they sell, here's what you'll find:

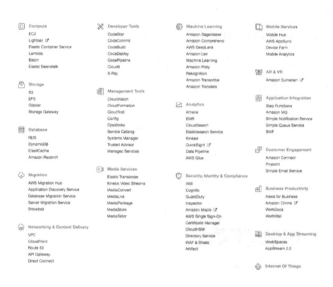

Take a look at the list. Each entry is a separate cloud service sold by Amazon. Google and Microsoft offer a similar, but not identical set of services in their clouds.

Don't worry, you don't have to understand what they all mean, we'll talk about a few of the services in just a moment, but you'll have to agree, that's a lot of services!

The key idea is this: **all of these AWS services run in the cloud**. The cloud is where cloud services run. Cloud services are not the cloud. We don't want to get the two ideas mixed up.

What does *run in the cloud* mean? Wherever software is used that's where it's *running*. Download an app onto your phone, click the icon to start it, that app is now running on your phone. In the same way, cloud services run in the cloud.

Let's try to understand the relationship between the cloud and cloud services through an analogy. Everyone shops for groceries, right?

The Cloud is Kind of Like a Grocery Store

When you need more milk, where do you go? This is not a trick question. You go to the grocery store.

Wikimedia Commons

A grocery store supplies groceries like bread, eggs, and lots of delicious candy. No particular item in a grocery store is the grocery store; the store is just where groceries are kept.

I know that seems silly to say, but I want to make the point that the cloud, cloud services, and cloud computing are different things.

Buying a cloud service is like buying groceries. When you need a cloud service you go the cloud service list we saw earlier and buy one. When you need groceries, you go to the grocery store and by them. There's no difference.

Cloud Storage Came First with S3 in 2006

If you look closely at the list of services, you'll see a section called Storage:

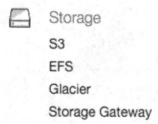

S3, which stands for *Simple Storage Service*, was the very first cloud service Amazon offered. The year was 2006. That year changed everything.

S3 is basically a big hard disk in the sky. Imagine a hard disk the size of infinity; S3 is almost that big.

You'll notice some other service names under Storage. EFS and Glacier are other kinds of storage services. S3 is the oldest and most important of them all.

In general, all the methods of storing data in the cloud is called *Cloud Storage.*

S3 became extremely popular for several reasons. S3 was: cheap, big, fast enough, extremely reliable, and easy for programmers to use.

Anyone could sign up to use S3 with just a credit card. Within minutes you could be storing huge amounts of data on S3. As we'll see, that sort of convenience was key to S3's success and AWS's success. Nothing like S3 had existed before.

Notice, we haven't talked about cloud computing yet. All we've talked about is cloud storage.

Cloud computing is just another service offered in the cloud, and in AWS at least, cloud computing came after cloud storage.

Cloud Computing Began with EC2 in 2007

If you look closely again at the list of services, you'll see a section called Compute:

Compute

EC2

EC2 Container Service

Lightsail ☐

Elastic Beanstalk

Lambda

Batch

EC2, which stands for *Elastic Compute Cloud,* was first made available to the public in 2007.

EC2 was the beginning of what we today call *Cloud Computing.* Remember when we talked about computer rental as a service in earlier chapters? That's cloud computing.

Cloud computing lets anyone with a credit card rent computers over the internet. That's it. Nothing fancy or intimidating

So far we've talked about cloud computing in enough detail that I think you have a good idea of what cloud computing is all about.

From here on out this chapter will get more technical. It's the most technical part of the whole book.

If you're interested in cloud computing then by all means proceed. Not that interested in cloud computing? You might want to skip to the next chapter.

I'm not trying to scare you off; I just don't want you to feel dejected if you get a little lost. If that's OK with you, then read on. We're going to talk about some interesting topics.

Still here? Good, let's get started.

Historically, services like EC2 had existed before, but EC2 was different in several important ways.

Software Developers Made AWS Successful

Before AWS, software developers suffered from a lot of limitations. EC2 washed those away. EC2 managed to hit a sweet spot with developers, and it was software developers who made S3, EC2 and thus AWS, successful.

Making developers happy is AWS's secret sauce; much in the same way making their online retail customers happy has made Amazon the dominant retail power in the US.

How did AWS make software developers happy? Let us count the ways.

EC2 is Easy to Use

Why did software developers like EC2 so much? Convenience. EC2, like S3, was super easy to use.

EC2 let anyone with a credit card and an internet connection rent computers on which they could run their own applications.

Need a computer? You could rent one within minutes. No hassle. No fuss. That's a genuine superpower.

EC2 is Permissionless

EC2 like S3 was *permissionless*. Renting a computer in minutes is great, but you know what's better? Not having to ask anyone for permission.

As a programmer, you didn't need to ask anyone in your company for permission before using EC2. EC2 didn't cost a lot, so almost any departmental budget could handle the expense without requiring a separate budgeting process. And if that didn't work, developers just paid for it themselves.

Isn't that crazy? Why would any developer pay for EC2 themselves?

It's hard today to understand what a revolution EC2 was. Back in the day if you needed a computer, it literally could take months for a computer to be purchased and installed in your datacenter. Literally, months.

New hardware often had to be approved by a committee. You might not even get all the hardware you asked for. Then a manager had to allocate funds from some budget. Then you had to wait for the purchasing department to cut a deal for the new computers. Then you had to wait for delivery. Then you had to wait for IT to make room in the datacenter and install everything.

As a software developer, this was torture. I'm a programmer and I can tell you waiting on long computer procurement cycles slows software development down to a crawl.

After all, what do software developers run their programs on? Computers. If you don't have computers there's not much you can do, is there?

Rather than fight the bureaucracy, developers turned to EC2. Using EC2 developers could "purchase" computers anytime they wanted.

Instant access to a rental pool of computers was a revelation for software developers. It meant they could develop software and release new features much faster. Software developers didn't need *permission* anymore.

With EC2 You Only Pay For What You Use

Imagine renting a car, and instead of paying a fixed rental fee you paid only for the miles you drove. Don't drive and the car costs you nothing. But surely, you don't have 24-hour access to the car? Yes, you do. The car sits ready to use in your driveway. Sounds good, doesn't it?

That's exactly how EC2 works. Need a computer for five hours, that's all you pay for. Back then you paid by the hour; recently Amazon changed so computer time on EC2 is paid by the second (with a one minute minimum).

This business model proved extremely popular with software developers. When EC2 first started an hour of computer time cost 10 cents. Those five hours of computer time only cost 50 cents. That's nothing. And for that price, you got a relatively powerful computer on which you could install and run any software you wanted. Now that same hour costs 4.64 cents. Nice.

The Cloud Advantage of OpEx vs. CapEx

Another angle on only pay for what you use is the operational expense (OpEx) vs. capital expenditure (CapEx) advantage. OpEx is the *ongoing cost for running a product, business, or system.* CapEx *are funds used by a company to acquire, upgrade, and maintain physical assets such as property, industrial buildings, or equipment.*

Traditionally computers are considered a capital expenditure. This is the budgeting process we talked about earlier.

Each calendar quarter you must succeed in getting a huge sum of cash approved upfront for all the computers you need for all the projects you're working on. Any computers purchased must come out of that budget.

Several problems with this process probably pop immediately into mind. First, how do you know how many computers you'll need in the future? Second, what if you're wrong? What if more computers than projected are needed?

You're out of luck. Your project suffers, and you fall behind schedule. Not good.

EC2 changes that whole dynamic. With EC2 you don't have to pretend you're Nostradamus. You just rent computers as you need them. AWS is on the hook for proper capacity planning. AWS is responsible for always making sure there are enough computers to rent. It's not your problem anymore.

The shift to cloud computing, renting computers in the cloud, meant the money for computers (and storage) came out of a completely different budget. Computers usage became an *operational expense.*

Moving costs to OpEx looks better on a company's balance sheet. Computers are expensive to buy and maintain. And you own those computers forever. For a business, that's a long-term investment on their balance sheet. It looks better for a business not to have long-term financial commitments on their books.

More importantly for software developers is the whole CapEx budgeting process is no longer needed. No upfront investment is needed to start a new project. When you need a computer, you rent it. Fast and simple.

With EC2 You Use Only What You Need

Now imagine you needed not one car, but 100 cars to take your extended family to a wedding. Can you instantly rent that many cars on-demand?

Unlikely. That's not how cars work. But that's how computers work. You can rent as many computers as you need in EC2 for as little time as you need.

The ability to cheaply rent as many computers as needed on-demand and then give them back when you're done with them **changed how software was made**.

That's not hyperbole. Since the introduction of the cloud, software development has not been the same. This new cloud-centric approach to developing software even has a name; it's called *Cloud Native*.

Cloud native means you architect your software so it can take advantage of the strengths and capabilities of the cloud.

To see how this came about, let's use Netflix as an example.

Netflix is fantastic service. It's growing incredibly fast, adding new users all the time.

Netflix has a problem. How can Netflix know how many computers it will need in the future? They can't. Nobody can. They must guess.

That's a problem.

Guess too low, Netflix won't have enough computers, and users will experience poor service.

Guess too high, Netflix will have a lot of extra equipment they don't need, and that wastes money.

If Netflix orders too little equipment one month can't they just order more next month? Yes, but Netflix is still guessing how many computers they need, so they're always chasing their tail. The problem is only made worse by how long it takes to order and install new equipment.

There's another problem that's less obvious. How does

Netflix change their software to make use of the new computers that are continuously being installed?

In practice, the difficulty of provisioning new hardware meant a software project was assigned a fixed number of computers. Those were all the computers you had so that's all the computers you built your software to handle. Reprogramming your software to handle more computers could take a long time.

Wouldn't it be better if Netflix could always have just the right number of computers?

Wouldn't it be better if Netflix could automatically have their software make use of new computers?

If you answered *yes* and *yes* then you're a genius. Pat yourself on the back.

This is exactly what EC2 allows software developers to do. And this is exactly what Netflix did. Netflix was an early EC2 adopter, and they're EC2's biggest success story.

They key is *elasticity*. Recall that the *E* in EC2 stands for *Elastic*. In case you were wondering what Elastic meant, and you were disappointed that I hadn't explained it, I was waiting for exactly this moment.

Elastic means you can add more computers when you need them and give them back when you don't need them anymore. Elastic means something can expand and contract.

It's like your favorite sweatpants with the elastic waistband on Thanksgiving. As you eat the elastic stretches with you. And when, well, you don't need the extra room the elastic shrinks back down.

AWS has a lot of computers available to rent. And it's their job to keep buying and installing new computers, so you don't have to.

This allowed Netflix to not worry about how many computers they had or would need. When more computers were needed, they could just rent more, confident AWS would have them available.

This is the *cloud native* software architecture we talked about earlier.

Netflix programs their software to automatically use more computers when it needs them. And when it doesn't need them it saves money by giving the computers back to Amazon to rent to someone else.

Netflix never has to change their software to make use of new computers. Their software automatically expands and contracts on its own.

EC2 is elastic. Netflix dynamically scales up and scales down their computer usage in response to demand. Netflix only pays for what they use. Netflix never orders, installs, or repairs computers themselves. This is what we know today as *cloud computing*.

Of course, the details are a lot more complicated, but this is the essence of how cloud computing works. Most new software today is built this way.

EC2 Increases Speed to Market

A huge benefit of EC2 for software developers is that they don't have to buy, build, install, repair, or replace anything.

Amazon does all that work, for a price of course, but most are more than willing to pay the price. Why?

Faster time to market. The software industry is very competitive. If you can beat a competitor by being first to market, then you have a huge competitive advantage.

By outsourcing all the infrastructure work to Amazon, you don't have to wait for IT to install new hardware. You also need fewer people in IT. And developers have a lot more time to program.

With more time to program software developers can concentrate on developing new services, releasing software faster, fixing more bugs, increasing quality, and adding new features.

Another way to put it is cloud computing increases *agility*. You can respond quicker to threats and take advantage of new opportunities.

In the cloud, there's much less friction getting in the way of starting new projects. Just assemble a small team, and you can start working on a new project immediately.

If a project fails it's no big deal; you aren't left with a data-center full of computers you still have to pay for. That's the advantage of not having CapEx on the books.

EC2 is Reliable

Computers that can fail at any time changes how software is made.

Historically, computers were built to be highly reliable. This meant software running on those computers usually didn't handle failure gracefully; the computers they ran on rarely failed.

EC2 changed all that. From the start, Amazon made it clear computers rented in EC2 could fail at any time. Your software had to deal with failure or else.

The reason is the kind of computers used in EC2. Those highly reliable computers are expensive. EC2 has hundreds of thousands of computers. There's no way they could afford to buy that many expensive, highly reliable computers. Instead, Amazon buys cheaper off-the-shelf computers.

Since the computers are cheap, Amazon buy lots of them, and since they're cheap, there's a higher chance they can fail.

Imagine your phone dropping in the middle of a phone call. That's what can happen to a computer in EC2 at any time.

It's important to understand that computers failing is not considered the exception. Computers failing in the cloud is the norm, it's expected, it's OK, and that changes how software is developed.

Your software must expect failure. If a computer fails, you should rent another one and restart your software on the new computer. The computer that failed is dead to you. It's gone. Don't worry about. There's always another computer in the cloud.

Another approach is to make your software run on multiple computers at the same time. Then if one or more computers fail, it won't affect service.

This is totally different than how software was written in the past. Software was written to work on a fixed set of computers that were assumed to be reliable.

That's why this new way of programming software was given a new name: *cloud native*. Cloud native software must be able to deal with computers failing at any time. The effect has been to make software much more flexible and reliable.

Datacenters can fail at any time.

Another driver for software being more reliable in the cloud is how the cloud makes it possible for programs to failover to a different datacenter when a disaster occurs. A disaster is something like a hurricane, flood, or power outage.

If you remember the *What is a Datacenter?* chapter, AWS has datacenters all over the world. Amazon divides the world into a 16 geographical regions. Within each region Amazon creates multiple availability zones (AZs). An availability zone consists of one or more datacenters.

One reason there are so many datacenters is so any given user will always be close to a datacenter. Another reason is reliability. By having multiple AZs in a region, which means having multiple datacenters in a region, if one datacenter fails another can take its place.

It's possible for a datacenter to fail. Datacenters do not fail often, but it does happen. The usual reason for a datacenter failing is not a big event like a hurricane. Usually, a datacenter fails from something as simple as a power failure.

If your software is running in a datacenter when it fails, what happens? Your software fails too. Then everyone will rush to

Twitter to complain about how unreliable and lousy your software is.

How does AWS handle datacenter failure? That's what the availability zones are for. AWS makes it possible to run software run in multiple AZs and even in multiple regions.

Historically, running software in multiple datacenters has been nearly impossible for small developers. Only the largest organizations could afford to do so.

Why? It's extraordinarily expensive to have multiple datacenters filled with equipment just in case one datacenter might fail. Who has that kind of money? Really large organizations. Everyone else? Not so much.

AWS has multiple datacenters. That means no additional CapEx is needed to make your software handle a datacenter level failure.

Is it easy to make software run in multiple AZs? Not at all. It's very difficult, but it's possible, and that's new with cloud computing.

Building a scalable and reliable service on other scalable and reliable services.

S3 is so reliable that if you store 10,000 files in S3 on average you can expect to lose one file every 10 million years. S3 was designed to withstand the concurrent loss of data in two separate storage facilities. That's reliable!

S3 is also scalable. You can store as much data as you want and remove it when you don't need it.

This is how all AWS services work. If you use AWS services in your program, then you can be assured your program will be reliable and scale as needed.

That's why Netflix uses S3 to store files. That's why Netflix uses Amazon's DynamoDB database to store data.

Building a program in the cloud means making it reliable and scalable. The easiest way to do that is to build your software on other services that are already reliable and scalable. That's another part of what it means to be cloud native.

Doesn't Cloud Computing have Downsides?

Yes, of course. Nothing is perfect. The trick is to decide what's important to you. Do the pros outweigh the cons?

Fortunately, the cloud is a spectrum; you can decide which services to adopt, which services to avoid, and just how much you want to commit to any given service.

Cloud computing is expensive.

This is the most common criticism of cloud computing, and it's also the most confusing.

Some assert cloud computing is too expensive and others assert they're adopting cloud computing specifically because it reduces their total cost of ownership (TCO).

Both can be equally true. The cloud can be expensive, and the cloud can be cheaper. It just depends. I hate *it depends* as an answer, but it applies here. It *depends*.

When doesn't it make sense to be in the cloud?

Dropbox is a perfect example. Dropbox started in AWS. Dropbox faced fierce competition in the storage market. By starting in AWS, Dropbox was able to build their platform and acquire customers without spending precious time and resources on building out an infrastructure. AWS managed the infrastructure for them. That meant Dropbox could concentrate on developing features quickly in order to find product/market fit.

Now Dropbox is established. They have a user base. They know what product they want to build. Which is why Dropbox is moving out of AWS. Dropbox is building their own custom infrastructure that is tailored to their exact needs. This will reduce costs, increase profitability, and allow them to better serve their customers.

If Dropbox had started by building out an infrastructure first, they would've failed. They wouldn't have known what to build because they wouldn't have known what their customers needed. And they wouldn't have been able to build customer-pleasing features because they would have spent all their time on infrastructure issues.

Netflix started in AWS and they're still in AWS, with no plans on leaving. Why? Because by leveraging AWS, Netflix can concentrate on building customer-pleasing features instead of infrastructure.

For Netflix, there's no competitive advantage in building their own datacenters. In fact, by using AWS Netflix was able to do something amazing. In 2016 Netflix went live in 130 countries simultaneously. This would have been impossible if Netflix had to build their own datacenters around the world before expanding. It would have taken years and billions of dollars to pull off. By using AWS Netflix was able to leverage the datacenter and cloud infrastructure AWS already had available.

Another important aspect to consider is Netflix charges real money for their service. Netflix can pay AWS for services because Netflix is getting paid too.

When adding new users increases revenues, you're not constrained by having to grow on the cheap. You can worry about getting stuff done in the best way possible.

If you're running a service with a lot of users and you aren't charging them, like many social networks startups these days, then the cloud is expensive. It's very expensive. You'd better have a lot of funding to pay for it.

But if you're making money on your service there's no competitive advantage to building and running your own datacenters. None.

Once upon a time companies had to build their own datacenters because public clouds like AWS simply did not exist.

Now, enterprises are moving to the cloud in droves. They realize there's no competitive advantage to running a datacenter anymore.

Coca-Cola, for example, processes transactions from its vending machines in AWS. A company the size of Coca-Cola obviously can afford their own datacenters, but they chose the cloud.

Why? Using the cloud is cheaper than building and managing their own datacenters, for this project at least. And using the cloud let's their developers spend more time on delivering valuable business projects. They don't have to worry about managing computers anymore.

Cloud computing costs are unpredictable.

This is true. In the cloud you pay for what you use, and that can bite you in any number of ways.

Let's say you simply underestimate how many resources your software will use. In that case, the cloud might be more expensive than predicted.

Let's say you have a traffic spike. You were expecting 1000 people a day to sign up for your new cloud-based recipe sharing service. Instead, 100,000 people a day signed up. Yay for you! But your costs would be a lot more than expected. And if you're not charging for your recipe sharing service the consequences could be disastrous.

Let's say your code has a bug that mistakenly increases how many resources you use. That will cost you.

Let's say you misuse a service. AWS, for example, has a bulk storage service called Glacier. It's super cheap. It's cheap because you promise not to access it very often. Access Glacier more than agreed, and it will cost you.

This is just a small sample of the many gotchas waiting for the unwary in the cloud.

Paying for being DDoSed (distributed denial-of-service attack).

Another risk is your service may be DDoSed. A DDoS occurs

when someone drives so much traffic to your site that it prevents other users from accessing your service.

With a pay as you go system handling all that useless traffic can cost a lot of money.

There are ways around this. You can throttle traffic. You can pay for a DDoS mitigation service. But no matter what you do, there's always a potential risk.

Paying for hidden expenses.

Another source of unpredictability in cloud computing are the hidden expenses that you didn't expect.

Cloud billing is complicated and hard to understand. It's not unusual to be surprised by large unforeseen expenses.

Let's say there's a bug in your code, and instead of starting five computers you made a typo and started 500 computers? That will cost you.

Let's say a file you thought would take 1 megabyte of storage in S3 actually took 1 gigabyte of storage, and you're storing millions of files. That will cost you.

Let's say you're downloading a lot of more files from S3 than expected. Data transfer out of AWS is expensive. That will cost you.

Let's say you miscalculated how much data your service will

store in DynamoDB, a database service offered by AWS. DynamoDB is expensive. That will cost you.

Let's say you have software running in multiple availability zones. The network traffic between AZs is not free. Use lots of bandwidth? That will cost you.

Paying for using a lot of services.

When developing software on AWS, you might find yourself using a lot more services than you thought. That's good. It saves a lot of work. It's bad since you have to pay for all those services. It adds up.

Paying for poor cloud hygiene.

A common problem on AWS is forgetting to clean up resources when you're done using them.

Let's say you start 500 computers and forget to stop them after the job they performed completed. Since those computers are still running, you're still paying for them. This can happen with disk space and lots of other AWS services. It can add up.

You have to keep a tight watch on all your expenses. Lots of things can cost you in the cloud. Cost optimization is almost a full-time job. You have to be smart in how you architecture your software and be as cloud native as possible.

Vendor lock-in creates dependency.

Lock-in means that it's hard to leave AWS once you start using all their services. You become dependent on them; like a drug. The more services you use, the harder it will be to move to some other service like GCP or Azure.

Why is lock-in a concern? What if AWS decides to raise prices? What if the services you use go to heck? If you want to move for whatever reason, it will take a huge amount of time, effort, and money.

This is true. There is lock-in. But there's always lock-in. You're locked into Facebook because all your family is on Facebook. Let's say, everyone where you work uses Microsoft Office and all your processes are built around Office. You're locked-in.

Lock-in isn't necessarily a bad thing. It means you're getting value. Yes, lock-in risk must be managed. Take steps to reduce your dependency on any services you use. Always have backup and transition plans. Structure your software so moving to a different cloud is possible.

Fear of lock-in should not paralyze you. You need to get stuff done, and if that requires a little lock-in, then that's almost always a fair price to pay.

You think you can do better than cloud providers.

The idea here is that if you build your own infrastructure, you can build something better than AWS, GCP, or Azure. You could buy better computers, build faster networks, and use faster hard drives. You could in general, just do better.

This is mostly false. True, some organizations can do better, but it requires a high level of skill and a lot of money.

That's not most of us. Most of us can't do better or can't afford to. So for most of us, AWS is more than good enough.

The cloud is not really secure.

This is false. AWS, for example, has a Secret Region operating workloads up to the Secret U.S. security classification level.

Immense resources are applied to make the cloud secure. It's far more secure than most people can build for themselves.

The cloud is not really reliable.

This is false. Everything fails. Every service suffers downtime. AWS will fail at times. One thing you know is they'll fix it as soon as possible.

And if minimizing downtime is really important to you then you would build your software to work in multiple availability zones. And if you really, really cared you would build your software to work across multiple regions.

Most people don't care that much. It's complicated and expensive to build really reliable software, so most of us accept a little downtime now and then as the price we pay for being able to concentrate on building software rather than infrastructure.

Most people are simply delusional to they think they can build infrastructure more reliable than AWS, GCP, or Azure. Some people can. Most of us can't.

Infrastructure as a Service (IaaS)

Infrastructure as a Service (IaaS) is a term you'll hear discussed in cloud computing circles, so it's something you should understand.

In fact, we'll also talk about PaaS (platform as a service), SaaS (software as a service), and serverless for the same reason.

These are subsets of cloud computing. They come up a lot when discussing the cloud and cloud computing.

Let's start with IaaS.

You know how the highway system is always being repaired? Datacenters are always being repaired too. Equipment breaks all the time and must be replaced. There's always more computers, more hard drives, and more networking devices to install.

Keeping a datacenter up and running 24x7 in a datacenter is a lot of work.

Who wants that kind of hassle? It's like when you rent a car; the rental agency is responsible for all car service and maintenance.

In the cloud, the service of taking care of all the infrastructure for you, became known as IaaS, or Infrastructure as a Service.

When you rent a computer using EC2 or storage through S3, you are using IaaS. Renting computers, renting storage, and managing all the infrastructure is the lowest level service the cloud can offer. That's IaaS.

Platform as a Service (PaaS)

PaaS is a level of service above IaaS. When using IaaS developers still have to do a lot of work to make an application. PaaS helps developers speed up development by doing a lot of the work for them.

Platform is kind of an odd word. A platform is something you can build other things on top of. Any PaaS offering must be a solid base on which to build applications.

If you think that's kind of vague, I agree. That's why I think there are two competing definitions of PaaS. I'll explain both of them.

Defining PaaS as a pure platform.

There's the idea of PaaS as a complete framework in which

developers build and deploy their applications. Examples are: Google App Engine and Heroku.

That probably won't make a lot of sense unless you're a software developer.

Let's try an analogy. Imagine you're hungry and you want to fix dinner.

So you figure out what you want to eat, you go to the store, buy all the ingredients, go home, cook it, eat it, and clean the dishes. That's IaaS.

Now let's say you signed up for one of those services that deliver a meal to your home for you to cook. It contains all the ingredients, but you do the cooking. That's PaaS.

Defining PaaS as a smorgasbord of services to choose from.

Another definition of PaaS is that it's a set of high-level services developers can choose from to build their applications. Examples are: databases, messaging, search, email, CDN (content delivery network), firewalls, load balancing, DNS, and so on.

If you don't know what all the above services are, that's OK. Let's take search as an example.

No doubt you've used Google search. Let's say we're building our own product, a Twitter clone, and we want to add search to it.

On IaaS developers can build their own search. The computers, storage, and network are all there to do it. The problem is it's really hard and time-consuming to build search into a program.

As a software developers you always have to ask this question when adding a new feature: is it a competitive advantage?

Is it a competitive advantage for our Twitter clone to have the best search in the world? Probably not, it's just something we must have. It's a checklist item.

So why build our own search? AWS offers a search service we can rent. It's called Elasticsearch. Is it great? Not really. Is it a little too expensive? Yes, definitely. But for a lot of projects that's OK. It's more important to get our Twitter clone in the hands of customers than it is to have the best and cheapest search feature.

Could Google use Elasticsearch? Absolutely not. It's not good enough, cheap enough, flexible enough, or scalable enough. For Google search is a key product differentiator, it's their main claim to fame, so Google must build the best possibly search they can. Google must build their own search product.

If you're not Google, and search is just another product

feature, using a pre-existing high-level service is a great way to make your product better and increase your speed to market.

AWS offers a lot of different services.

Let's say our Twitter clone wants to add a dash of AI, but our developers aren't experts in machine learning, and they don't have time to learn, and we can't afford to hire AI experts. That's a perfect use case for PaaS. And it just so happens AWS offers AI services. Imagine that!

 Machine Learning

Amazon SageMaker

Amazon Comprehend

AWS DeepLens

Amazon Lex

Machine Learning

Amazon Polly

Rekognition

Amazon Transcribe

Amazon Translate

Like for IaaS, the cloud provider does all the work in supporting PaaS. The developer doesn't have to do anything. They just use the service and pay the fee.

Software as Service (SaaS)

One level above PaaS is Software as a Service or SaaS. Ordering a pizza delivered to your house, that's SaaS.

With SaaS, developers are not involved, customers use a full-blown software product, not a service used in building some other product.

That's worth repeating. Both IaaS and PaaS are services used by developers to build products. No end user will ever use IaaS or PaaS directly. They are exclusively for developers.

SaaS is meant for end users to use directly.

A great example of SaaS from Microsoft is Office 365. Once upon a time you may have purchased Microsoft Word, Microsoft Excel, and their whole Office Suite on a CD and installed it on your computer at work or home.

Not anymore. Microsoft offers Office in the cloud now. They call it Office 365. For a yearly fee, you can use Office over the internet as a service. You don't have to install anything, maintain anything, upgrade anything, or do anything but use it. Microsoft does all the work for you.

That's what SaaS is, software rented and used over the internet. You don't typically buy SaaS software, it's subscription based. Like a magazine, you pay monthly or yearly.

Other examples of SaaS are: Salesforce, Quickbooks Online, Gmail, Google Apps, Zendesk, DocuSign, Slack, and DropBox.

And just like with IaaS and PaaS, with SaaS you don't do any maintenance. Everything is taken care of for you. That's why you pay the big bucks for SaaS.

Will a SaaS product be implemented in a cloud like AWS? You don't know. All you see is the user interface; you know very little about how the software is implemented on the back-end. You assume it's reliable, secure, scalable, and is backed-up regularly, but you don't know.

Salesforce, a customer relationship management product, runs their own datacenters. That makes sense for them. Salesforce is a huge established business. They have the resources to do everything for themselves.

Slack, a team messaging product, uses AWS because they are a startup. Slack wants to get as many customers as fast as possible. This means they want to concentrate on developing features rather building out infrastructure.

Evolution of Cloud Computing: VMs to Containers to Serverless

Cloud computing has undergone an evolution. Cloud

computing started with VMs, then containers were developed, and now serverless is the new hot thing.

Don't know what any of that means? Don't worry; we're going to cover it right now. Let's walk through the changes. It might help to put an image like one of those human evolution pictures in your mind:

EC2 Started Sharing Computers Using Virtual Machines

Throughout this book, I've said what you're renting in the cloud is a computer. That's a bit of a simplification. It's more accurate to say what you're renting in EC2 is a VM (virtual machine). AWS calls these *instances*. A VM is an instance of a computer.

You'll often hear *server* used instead of VM or instance. In fact, you'll hear phrases like *renting a server* more often than anything else. *Server* is just a cooler way to say computer.

A server in the cloud looks something like:

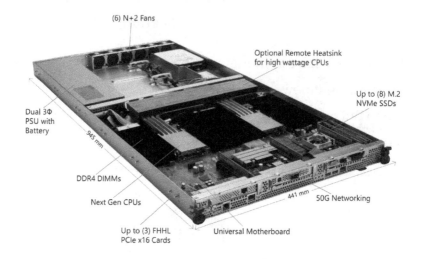

Microsoft

Another simplification is that when you rent a server in the cloud, you don't actually rent the whole thing. How and why you only rent part of a server in the cloud is what we'll cover next.

What is a Virtual Machine (VM)?

If you can only rent part of a server in the cloud, there must be some way for programs to share a computer. That's where virtual machines (VMs) come in.

A VM allows many programs to run on one computer at the same time. VMs are how big, powerful computers are shared.

"What's the big deal?" you say, a lot of programs are running on my computer right now. The difference is using a VM, each program thinks it has total and complete control of the entire computer. It can install its own operating system, run any number of other programs, access the hard disk, access the network, do anything it wants, just like it's running on the computer all by itself.

I like to show pictures of new things to help you better understand them. That's hard with VMs because they're pure software. They don't look like anything. Not only can't I find a good picture, I can't even come up with a good analogy. Virtual machines are like nothing else in the world.

A VM is like Airbnb where everyone can stay at the same time.

Let's try an analogy anyway. It's not perfect, but I hope it gets the point across.

Are you familiar with Airbnb? Airbnb helps homeowners make money by renting out their homes when they aren't using them.

Only one renter can rent a home at a time.

Now imagine 1000 renters sign up to rent a house and they all show up at the same time. There would be a lot of angry Airbnb customers!

Now imagine the homeowner knows a bit of magic. The homeowner casts a spell making each renter think they are alone in the house. Each renter lives in their own separate dimension.

Never does one renter see or interfere with another renter. Each thinks they have the house to themselves.. They can invite friends over. They can move furniture around. They can have a BBQ on the back porch. They can fill up the refrigerator with groceries. No renter knows or can possibly know the other renters are there at the same time.

Now that's some strong magic. In computers we call that magic *virtualization*. Virtual means *not physically existing as such but made by software to appear so*. Hence virtualization means *the act of creating a virtual (rather than actual) version of something*.

Each renter thinks they have an actual real house, but in fact, what they have is a virtual house. Does it matter to the renter if the house real or virtual? Not at all. They can't tell the difference.

Think what a financial windfall this is for the homeowner. They pay for one house, yet they can rent it out to a thousand people a night!

It's great for renters too. They each get access to a very nice house, cheaper than they ever could before.

A VM is a slice of a computer.

The above is exactly how VMs work. A VM is a slice of a computer that behaves exactly like a *bare-metal* computer.

Bare-metal means you're directly using a computer's hardware. The desktop computer you use at work or home is a *bare-metal* computer. It's likely all the computers you've ever used are bare-metal computers because as consumers that's what we use.

In the cloud, bare-metal computers are not the norm. Instead, in the cloud, computers are shared using virtualization. Tens, hundreds, or even thousands of programs run on the same computer in the cloud at the same time.

VMs insert a software layer above a bare-metal computer that fools programs into sharing a computer without them knowing they're sharing.

A virtual machine pretends to be a full computer, but it's not. A VM is really just a small slice of a computer. Programs can't notice the difference between a bare-metal computer and a VM. Each program running in a VM thinks it has a bare-metal computer all to itself.

Why not just give every program its own computer?

Because computers these days are very powerful. It's almost

impossible for any single program to completely use all the power modern computers have to offer.

Before VMs computers mostly sat idle. These very expensive computers literally had nothing to do, so they did nothing. That's inefficient and a waste of money.

That's why VMs were invented. VMs make it possible to fully utilize all of a computer's resources. How? By packing as many programs as possible onto each computer.

Here's how it works. If you put a program in its own virtual machine, it thinks it's running on a real computer. That means you can run a large number of VMs on a single bare-metal computer without any of the programs knowing the difference.

As long as no program knows the difference, does it really matter if you're running on a VM or a real computer? No, it doesn't. No more than it did in our Airbnb example.

So you can just keep adding VMs to a computer until you reach some maximum load. The problem of having idle computers disappears. With so many VMs running on a computer the computer always has something to do. That's efficient. We're using our very expensive computers as much as physically possible.

The real genius of the cloud: selling previously

unused computer capacity.

If bare-metal computers mostly sit idle, can you imagine how much unused capacity there must be in hundreds of thousands of computers?

All that unused computer capacity must be worth a fortune, if you could package it up and resell it. It would be like having a spare nuclear power plant in your backyard with no power grid over which you could sell electricity to other homes and businesses.

Wait, can't we use VMs to make use of all this unused capacity? Bingo!

Cloud computing succeeded because VMs allowed previously unused computer capacity to be repackaged and resold.

Exploiting unused computer capacity using VMs is exactly how and why AWS makes so much money.

AWS is like a nuclear power plant and a power grid for distributing access to computers.

Cloud customers get an advantage too. Because computers are being shared, the cloud is relatively cheap to use.

Containers: Run Even More Programs on a Computer

Containers evolved after VMs and are even better at sharing computers because they use fewer resources. Since containers use fewer resources than VMs, it's possible to pack even more applications on a bare-metal computer.

What's the difference between a container and a VM? It's complicated. I'm going to try to explain the difference, but don't feel bad if you don't get it. It's not that important to understand the differences anyway.

The job of a VM is difficult. It must pretend to be a full computer, so it has to look like a computer. This means a VM must make a complete copy of the OS (operation system) that runs the computer and complete virtual copy of all the hardware the OS needs to run.

What's an operating system? Every computer runs a program called an operating system. An OS manages everything on the computer. If you've used Windows, Mac OS, iOS, or Linux, those are operating systems.

Operating systems are large. They take up a lot of memory, disk space, and use a lot of CPU. That's why making a copy for every VM uses a lot of resources.

Containers were invented to get the same result as VMs, but use fewer resources in the process. A container allows programs to share a computer just using the OS. The OS knows how to make every program think it has the computer completely to itself. This means all containers can share one OS, so a separate copy isn't needed.

Containers are so efficient at letting programs share a computer that two to three times more applications can share a computer using containers compared to VMs.

As you might imagine packing more programs on a computer excites cloud providers a lot.

But we can do even better. That's serverless.

Serverless: Cheapest and Easiest of them All

We started off by thinking of cloud computing as renting computers in the cloud. Then we said what people are really renting are slices of computers using VMs. Then we said you could rent even smaller slices of a computer using containers.

Serverless takes renting smaller slices of a computer to the next level. With serverless, instead of running a complete application in a VM or a container, you upload a function into a serverless service and it takes care of everything else.

Serverless has been a revolutionary change in cloud computing, as big as EC2 was back in its day. Serverless has been a smash hit with developers and enterprises alike.

What's driving serverless adoption? Serverless is simpler and cheaper for developers. At the same time, serverless increases server utilization and thus yields higher profits for cloud providers.

That's a powerful combination. Let's dive deeper.

The most popular serverless service is AWS Lambda.

AWS released Lambda in 2014. AWS wasn't first to market with serverless, but they have been the most successful by far.

Microsoft has their own serverless service; it's called Azure Functions. Google also has their own serverless service; it's called Google Cloud Functions.

What's a function?

A function is a chunk of code written in a programming language that tells a computer exactly what to do.

All the apps you use are built from a bunch of functions. The more complicated an app is, the more functions it will have. Computers aren't that smart. It takes a lot of functions to get them to do anything interesting.

With serverless, you don't run a complete app (or program).

You run a single function.

A function is simple enough that I can even show you an example:

```
exports.myHandler = function(event, context, callback)
{

console.log("here's an example function!");

// do stuff

callback(null, "some success message");

}
```

This is a really simple function written in Javascript that does nothing interesting, but it is an example of the kind of code that you could upload into in a serverless service.

By *upload*, I mean the same thing as when you upload a picture to Instagram or a movie to YouTube. The function source code is copied into the serverless service.

What does a serverless service do for you?

Lots. The main thing a serverless service does is after uploading a function, it runs your function in response to a request or an event.

A *request* asks for some job to do be done. An example is telling Netflix to play a video. You can create a function to handle any request imaginable.

An *event* is a notification something happened. An example is a file being added to S3. The are many kinds of events that can cause serverless functions to run. This is why you'll sometimes hear that serverless is *event-driven*. Events are often used to trigger serverless functions to run.

Serverless is simpler.

The magic of serverless is your function just runs.

The serverless service finds a computer, copies your function to it, and runs it automatically. You do nothing.

If more requests come in or more events fire, the serverless service automatically starts more of your functions to handle the load. There's effectively no limit to how many functions can be started.

Why is this simpler? You don't rent computers anymore. You don't have to worry about VMs or containers. You no longer have to deal with capacity planning, deploying software, installing software, patching software, or elastically scaling in response to demand.

You're free from all that extra overhead. All you do is create and upload functions. You don't even have to worry about failures like you do with EC2.

No paying for idle-time.

When a function completes you're done paying for it. You only pay for a function while it's running.

As an example, let's say you have a website for your recipe sharing service. What if nobody using your service? This is called *idle-time*.

On IaaS you would need a VM running all the time to handle any requests that might come in. Even if there were no requests to process, you still must pay for at least one VM.

With serverless you don't need a VM, so you're not paying for a VM. When a request from your recipe sharing services comes in, then and only then will your function to be started to handle the request. And since you only pay for functions while they are running, you never pay for idle-time.

This adds up to huge savings.

Serverless is cheaper.

Compared to containers and VMs, many more serverless functions can be packed onto each computer.

This brings the cost of running serverless functions down because it increases the utilization of each server.

Coca-Cola loves serverless.

Remember our Coca-Cola example from earlier? Coca-Cola handles all their vending machine transactions in the cloud. What I didn't tell you is they do it using AWS Lambda.

Coca-Cola loves serverless and Lambda. So much so that they now mandate serverless solutions or require a justification for why you won't use serverless.

Why so much serverless love? Look at the numbers.

It's fast. Each vending machine transaction happens in under a second.

It's cheap. Coca-Cola estimates serverless is nearly 3x cheaper than IaaS. Each transaction only costs them 1/1000 of a penny.

It's good business. Coca-Cola says serverless lets them focus better on delivering business value. Using IaaS only 39% of their time was spent delivering business projects. After moving to serverless, it was 68%.

Not having to worry about servers removes a lot of the grunt work associated with IaaS.

Serverless is for developers.

Like IaaS and PaaS, serverless is targeted directly at software developers. Serverless is a service programmers use to build other services. End users never see it.

Serverless is the same FaaS (Functions as a Service).

You might hear Serverless called FaaS, or Functions as a Service. The mean the same thing and are used interchangeably.

Does serverless have any downsides?

Yes, of course.

One of the difficulties is that serverless uses functions. Functions tend to be small and simple, so you need to use of lot of cooperating functions to get things done. This is tricky for programmers to both code and manage. Serverless is so new this isn't a solved problem yet.

Another problem is what's called *cold-start* latency. If a request comes in for your function and there's not one already running, it can take a while to copy your function to a server and start it running.

There are more downsides that are too technical for us to get into here. Are any of them deal-killers? Not so far.

Is serverless the future?

Many think IaaS, VMs, and containers have merely served as

a transition phase to the future and that future is serverless computing. They just might be right.

Public Cloud vs. Private Cloud

We've mostly talked about *public clouds* so far. AWS, GCP, and Azure are public clouds. Anyone can use them.

What if you want to build your own cloud in your own data-centers? That's called a *private cloud*.

There are several reasons a company might want a private cloud.

Usually, enterprises build private clouds because they want the advantages of using a cloud infrastructure, but they want complete and total control of their environment.

A business might be concerned about security and privacy. If you have sensitive data, then you may not want the risk of storing it in a public cloud.

A business might use special hardware that's not available in the public cloud.

A business might have huge amounts of data, so it's not practical or cost efficient to move all that data into a public cloud.

A business might already have their own services running in their own datacenters, yet they'd like to start developing new services in the cloud. In that case, it makes sense to keep their new cloud as close as possible to their existing services. That would make it much easier to integrate the two together.

There are not many private cloud offerings. The reason is it turns out to be really hard to build a cloud. It takes a great deal of expertise that most companies simply do not have.

Microsoft sells a private cloud product as do RedHat, VMware, and IBM.

That's about all I have to say on private clouds. You should be aware they exist and are an option. In general, choose a public cloud when possible.

Creating your own private cloud sounds like a great idea, but private clouds are a lot harder to build than you might think.

We've come to the end of our whirlwind tour of cloud computing. I tried to introduce all the major ideas and explain what they mean without getting too technical. That's not always easy. Just let me know if there are any other topics you'd like me to cover or explain better.

17

THE GOOD, THE BAD AND THE UGLY OF CLOUD SERVICES

I've talked up the cloud quite a bit so far, but the cloud is not perfect. It has advantages and disadvantages. Let's take a look at some of them.

The Good

Cloud Storage is Safe

One benefit of storing stuff in a storage unit is that if your house burns down the stuff in the storage unit is safe.

The same is true for stuff stored in the cloud. Lose your phone, and your stuff still exists in the cloud. Get a new phone, and your stuff comes back. If your data existed only on your phone, that would not be possible; the data would be lost when the phone was lost.

Cloud Storage is Infinite

Cloud storage is effectively infinite. Your cloud provider adds new storage units all the time. While your device has a storage limit, the cloud does not. Of course, you do have to pay for it.

The Cloud is Available from Any Device at Anytime

We've talked about how this works a few times. Cloud storage and cloud services are accessible from any device at any time of the day or night.

Cloud Storage is Permanent

Storing stuff in the cloud has another advantage. It's permanent. It's stupendously hard to lose data in the cloud, but not impossible. Accidents do happen. Always make backups, even if your data is in the cloud.

A first class cloud service stores your data in at least three different geographical locations. If disaster strikes one data-center, your data will still be available from one of their other datacenters.

Remember how we said cloud providers had to have deep pockets? This is one reason why. It's very expensive to replicate data across all those datacenters, but as a result, your data isn't going anywhere.

There are two more common reasons why you may lose data: *you delete it*, or *you don't pay your bill*.

You delete it. Delete your data; it's gone. That's obvious enough.

You don't pay your bill. Most cloud services charge monthly or yearly fees. Stop paying your bill, or your credit card expires, the service goes away, and your data disappears.

The Cloud is Secure (Mostly)

There has always been a lot of FUD (fear, uncertainty, and doubt) thrown around saying cloud services are insecure. The question is always: insecure compared to what? Insecure compared to your home computer? Insecure compared to your office computer? Insecure compared to your laptop?

It's highly doubtful, unless you work for a company that takes security very, very seriously, that any of the computers you use will be as secure as computers rented from a top notch cloud provider. Google, Amazon, Microsoft, all employ armies of people constantly monitoring their cloud for security breaches. They're experts at security, and they have the time and money to do it right.

For example, AWS is PCI Level One Compliant, meaning

the physical infrastructure has been audited and approved by an authorized, independent Qualified Security Assessor. All the top level clouds meet similar stringent security standards.

How about other clouds or other cloud services? That's less clear. Security is tremendously difficult and expensive to do right. Software can always have bugs. People can always make mistakes. But unless you're the NSA or have special requirements, I wouldn't spend a lot of time worrying about if cloud services like Google Drive or QuickBooks Online are secure. They are.

When you get to second tier services, especially those that are free or very cheap, I would worry more. Always do your due diligence. Always do your research. Always ask a service to explain how it handles security. They should be able to tell you, and if not, stay away. But when it comes to top tier clouds and services, the odds are that they will be far more secure than anything you could build yourself.

Subscription Based Cloud Services are a Better Business Model

Paying once for a program is a lousy business model. It puts a lot of financial pressure on a business. Programming, releasing, supporting, fixing and updating software is expensive.

Users expect a company to support a program, provide bug

fixes and add new features forever. There's just one problem: where does the money come from for all that work?

You've already paid for the program. No more money is coming from you. New sales can finance development costs for awhile, but sales eventually slow down. What then?

That's when businesses feel the pinch. Users will complain about a lack of bug fixes, a lack of new features, yet they'll scream bloody murder if they're charged for a new release.

It's a death spiral. A healthy business requires a constant stream of revenue to finance new development.

Since cloud services are almost always subscription based, they are assured of a predictable revenue stream. With that predictability they can hire people, buy equipment, rent facilities, build new features, improve performance, improve reliability, and they can commit to releasing updated software on a regular schedule.

Who likes paying monthly for a service? Nobody. But it works out best for everyone.

Cloud Apps Can Have Far More Powerful Features

We often think of desktop programs as more powerful than their app and web cousins. Features usually drop when a desktop program shrinks to fit inside an app or web interface. Everything is streamlined and simplified, often to the dismay of desktop users who miss the power of the old version.

What we're learning is **desktop programs are not always more powerful**. Cloud services can be significantly more powerful. Why? The resources available in the cloud dwarf the resources of any desktop computer.

Let's bring back our QuickBooks Online example, as, well, an example.

QuickBooks Online can automatically link bank and credit card accounts. With a single click, transactions import automatically into bank account registers.

Another improvement of the online version is you can create "Bank Rules" instructing QuickBooks how to categorize certain transactions. For instance, an electronic transfer of more than $600 that includes "Ford" in the description, can automatically be setup to be entered as a car lease payment. That saves a ton of work.

We're mobile beings these days. When you combine the ability of online services to be accessed from anywhere with the power of mobile computers like your phone, entire new capabilities open up. When you're on the road, for example, you can capture receipts using your phone's camera and upload them using QuickBooks mobile app. That's a feature you could never even dream of when using the desktop version.

There are still some areas where the desktop version is more appropriate, like job costing and inventory for certain manufacturing situations. But the online version is quickly improving. Before long, the online version will surpass the desktop version.

The Bad

Cloud Services Close Down

Want to know a dirty little secret? Yes, of course you do. Cloud services can disappear overnight.

Nirvanix was a cloud storage provider that went out of business with little or no notice. Sadly, many customers weren't able to transfer their data out in time. Megacloud was another online storage company that suddenly went bust. It can and does happen.

It's also possible for a service to close down because it was bought by another company. The buyer may choose to shutdown the service, or keep it going; it depends on their goals.

My favorite service in the whole world—FriendFeed—was bought by Facebook and brutally shutdown. It was a sad day. I still miss my old FriendFeed friends.

Regardless of why a service closes down, you might not have a chance to recover your data. All of it could be lost.

Cloud Storage Can Be Expensive

Usually, cloud storage has a low entry cost plan to get you hooked. Apple's iCloud, for example, gives you the first 5GB for free. Then, 50GB, at the time of this writing, is $.99 a month. That's $12 a year. 200 GB is $36 a year. 2TB is $120 a year.

Apple's prices are higher than most cloud storage providers. And 50GB may seem like a lot of storage, but keep in mind, every picture takes megabytes of storage. Recording videos at 4K resolution is a huge storage hog. And don't forget all the movies and music you keep downloading. Backing up your iPhone and iPad also takes up a lot of space.

Storage usage always increases. Each picture, each video, each song, requires more storage. The problem: storage isn't paid for just once. You pay for it, every year, basically forever.

Do you even need cloud storage? Not always. If you buy a 128GB iPhone, you can use that storage for free. You've already paid for it. Just keep taking pictures, at least until you run out of storage. And that's the problem. Data must be deleted to reclaim space. If you're using the cloud, all you have to do is buy more cloud storage.

The Cloud Can Be Slow

Let's say you want to view a photo. Which do you think will display faster, a photo stored on your device or a photo stored in the cloud? Depending on your network, it can be very slow to access the cloud over the internet. You've probably been in a place that had slow Wi-Fi. It's hell. In contrast, accessing a photo from your device is always consistently fast.

Usually, accessing your stuff over the internet works just fine, but when it doesn't, it can be maddening. What a lot of programs do is store a local copy of your most recently used data on your device. It only goes to the cloud when there's a request for something not already on your device. Apple Photos works this way. Not every app does because it's hard to program correctly.

In the end, your cloud service is only as fast as your internet connection. If you plan to travel in locations with a slow or unavailable internet connection, then you may want to use an app that isn't based on a cloud service.

The Cloud Can be Unavailable

This is a variation of *The Cloud can Be Slow*. Sometimes the internet is not available. Maybe you can't find Wi-Fi, or maybe you have zero bars on your cell service, which means, your cloud services will not be available either. That's the advantage of using programs that work only on your device; they work anywhere, it doesn't matter if you have an internet connection or not.

There are ways to work around the lack of an internet connection. Some apps can use the local device and then, when the internet comes back up, they'll sync whatever you did back to the cloud. Facebook Messenger will do this. You can send texts even when there's no cell connection, and when it comes back up, it will send your texts. Some apps, like Google Maps, can download a big area of the map to your device, so you can use it to navigate even when there's no internet connection. That's unusual though. And even Google only recently made this no internet connection version of Google maps.

The Ugly

It's Easy for Governments to Get Your Data

When your data is in the cloud, it's easy for law enforcement and the government to get your data without you even knowing it. All they need is a subpoena, and the cloud provider is required to give up your data. Just something to keep in mind.

Free Services May Sell Your Data

Running a cloud service is expensive. If you're not being charged for a service, you have to ask yourself, why? How are they paying for it? There are three potential answers to that question: *startups burning through cash, selling data for dollars,* and *using data for dollars.*

Startups burning through cash.

One possibility is the cloud service is a startup trying to sign up as many users as possible, as fast as possible. They offer the service for free with the intention of charging for it later. This is the kind of service that can close down or get bought by a larger company, so be careful. Don't rely on this kind of service too heavily and make sure your data is backed up. If a startup goes out of business, they may sell your data as a way of making some money back for investors.

Selling data for dollars.

Unroll.me is a service that helps keep your inbox clean by unsubscribing from email lists. A useful service for a lot of people. To know which email lists you have joined, they need to read all the email in your inbox. This should scare you right away. Letting anyone read your email is a potential security nightmare. But if you like the service, it may be worth it. What Unroll.me failed to clearly tell users is they were selling data from customer inboxes. Uber, for example, bought information on how many people were using Lyft. How did Unroll.me know this? They read your inbox. If you use Lyft, your inbox probably has a receipt from any transactions, so they just keep track.

AccuWeather, one of the most popular weather apps in Apple's app store, is another example of an app selling user data without explicit consent. AccuWeather sent geolocation data to a third-party firm to be used by advertisers, even when location sharing was switched off.

Using data for dollars.

Google offers a massively popular free email service called Gmail. It's a great service. They don't sell your data to others, but they do use your data to show you targeted ads. That's how they keep Gmail "free." How do we know they don't sell your data? We don't really. We just "trust" Google. In this kind of arrangement you always have to ask yourself: do I trust them? Most of us trust Google...for now. Be glacially slow to trust an unknown service provider.

The rule is: If you're not paying for a service then beware. They have to make money somehow. One way to make money is to sell your data, which could be a huge violation of your privacy. Even if you are paying for a service, read their privacy statement to see what they are doing with your data. They can still sell your data, even if you are paying for the service. Move on if you don't like their privacy policy. There's always another service in the sea.

18

KINDLE: AMAZON'S CLOUD SERVICE FOR READING EBOOKS

Are you already reading ebooks on Kindle? If so, this will be a great example of a cloud service for you. If not, let me take a quick detour and explain how ebooks work.

What are ebooks? They are electronic versions of a printed book that you read on a device. If you recall our discussion of data, an ebook is just a regular book turned into data. Once a book is turned into data then an app can read it on any device. If that doesn't make sense right now, hopefully, it will in a bit.

In 2007 Amazon introduced a device for reading ebooks called the Kindle. Here's a picture of one:

Wikimedia Commons

Amazon was not first to market with an e-reader device like the Kindle, but they were able to transform ebooks into a big business. The secret sauce was Amazon's online bookstore.

With Amazon's online bookstore authors didn't need to create a paper version of their book anymore. Instantly accessing an audience of millions of book buyers became as easy as uploading an electronic version of your book. Combine the ease of creating new books with Amazon's book selling expertise, and the self-publishing boom was born.

Now customers can search for a book, buy it, download it to their Kindle, and begin reading in a few minutes. Convenience won the day, and Amazon now dominates ebook sales.

Amazon also built a Kindle app for Apple and Android devices. Using the Kindle app, you don't need to buy a Kindle device to read ebooks from Amazon. Download the free Kindle app, and you can instantly read almost any book you want.

Kindle is a Cloud Service

OK, we've described what Kindle is. Why do we care? Kindle is a cloud service. When you buy and download an ebook, the whole process uses a service running in Amazon's cloud.

Kindle is a perfect example of a cloud service because the Kindle app itself has two different views of the ebooks you've bought: a *cloud view* and a *device view*.

Cloud View

All the ebooks you've ever bought on Amazon are available in the cloud view.

Let's look at what the cloud view looks like in my Kindle app:

You know Kindle is in the cloud view because it tells you. I've conveniently circled the current view in yellow.

All the images are of book covers. Each cover is a book I've bought. Over the years I've bought hundreds of books, and I can look through all of them here. Remember, the cloud has infinite storage, so no matter how many books you buy, the cloud can handle it.

What can't handle storing all my books? My iPad. Storage is

limited on my iPad. The solution is to download to my iPad only the books I'm reading right now. That's the device view.

Device View

Only ebooks you've downloaded to your device are available in the device view.

Here's what my device view looks like:

See, not many books are stored on my iPad, just the ones I'm currently reading. Tap a book cover in the device view, and you're instantly reading the book.

Downloading a book from the cloud is easy. In the cloud view just tap on the cover picture and it downloads to your device. Switch over to the device view and the book will be there.

After I finish reading a book, I remove it from my device. Removing a book from your device doesn't delete the book forever. You still own it. You can always download the book again from the cloud view. Your books are always available from Amazon's cloud.

Why does Kindle go through all the effort of keeping a cloud and device view?

Two reasons: *limited device storage* and *reading without an internet connection*.

Limited device storage.

Your device has a limited amount of storage space. You can only download so much data before your device becomes full.

It's possible the number of books you own can be far larger than the number of books that can fit on your device.

You need a way of viewing all the books you've ever

purchased. That's the cloud view. No matter how many books you own they'll show up in the cloud view.

You also need to be able to read any book you want at any time. That's the device view. You can download just the books you want to read on your device. That way you won't run out of room on your device because you don't need to keep all your books on your device.

You can manage the amount of space used on your device by only downloading the books you are currently reading and immediately deleting books from your device when you are done reading them. Using this strategy even small amounts of storage can be more than enough.

Reading without an internet connection.

When I go to the beach, there's no internet connection, yet I can still read books on my iPad. How does that work?

In the cloud view, as long as you have an internet connection, you can download any book on to your device.

When you download a book from the cloud it is now physically stored on your device. Kindle can read the book directly from your device. This means you don't need an internet connection to read a book that has been downloaded to your device. You can go anywhere you want and read. No internet connection required.

Cloud Services Enable More Cool Features

Kindle remembers where you are in a book.

Let's say you're comfy in your living room reading a book on your iPad. You feel like going out, so you get a coffee at Starbucks, but you don't want to bring your big iPad.

Your book was just getting good, so while drinking coffee, you pull out your iPhone and start reading the same book from exactly the same spot you left off reading on your iPad, even though they are two completely different devices.

Kindle remembers where you are in each book. It stores your last reading position as data in the cloud. When you resume reading, Kindle asks the cloud for your last reading position. That's how it knows where you are in the book.

Kindle remembers highlighted passages.

As you're reading, you can highlight any passage from a book. When you read the book on a different device, Kindle will *remember which passages you highlighted*, so those passages will be highlighted on every device. How does that work? It's another cloud service.

You can also see the *most highlighted passages* in a book. If a lot of people highlight the same passage Kindle will notice and show it to you while you're reading. Yep, that's another cloud service.

Kindle takes notes.

Kindle also has a *notes feature.* You can write notes to yourself while reading. By now you know what I'm going to say: any notes you make on one device will be available on any other device you use to read the same book. How? If you said it's a cloud service, then you're right!

All these Kindle features—remembering where you are in a book, remembering highlighted passages, knowing the most highlighted passages, and remembering notes— would be impossible without the cloud.

Think about it. Without the cloud, how could a book on one of your devices know about the same book on another of your devices? How could it possibly know when someone is reading the same book in a completely different country?

There's no way these devices could exchange this kind of data because there's no way they could know about each other's existence.

But since Kindle is a cloud service, all these cool features are possible.

That's the power of the cloud.

19

ICLOUD: APPLE'S CLOUD SERVICE FOR SYNCING DATA

If you're an iPhone or an iPad user then the cloud you're probably most familiar with is Apple's iCloud.

According to Apple, iCloud: *securely stores your photos, videos, documents, music, apps, and more — and keeps them updated across all your devices. So you always have access to what you want, wherever you want it.*

Here's what my iCloud looks like over the web:

My experience is people have a hard time understanding what iCloud does, which makes sense, because iCloud is confusing. The reason iCloud works differently from other cloud services has to do with Apple's business model. Yes, their business model.

Apple's Business Model Dictates their Cloud Architecture

How does Apple make money? It sells hardware devices like the iPhone, iPad, MacBook, Watch and the iMac.

It's not hard to imagine Apple would like you to buy more of their phones, tablets, laptops, watches, and desktop computers. But ask yourself what would happen if all the services Apple offered were performed in the cloud and not on an Apple device?

Well, you wouldn't need an Apple device to use the service, would you? That means you wouldn't buy as much Apple hardware and Apple wouldn't make as much money. We can't have that, can we?

Apple Uses a Device Centric Model

Apple's approach to the cloud is different because *Apple uses a device centric model instead of a cloud centric model*. Apple wants the experience of using their devices to be seamless and consistent. They don't want data compartmentalized on each device.

Add a contact on your iPhone and Apple wants that contact to be on your iPad the next time you use it. If that contact weren't on your iPad, you'd be angry, which isn't the kind of experience Apple wants you to have.

Apple makes all your devices work together by syncing data between them. *Sync* means keep synchronized, meaning a change on one device is reflected on all your other devices. Delete a contact on one device, and it's deleted everywhere. Add a contact, and it's added everywhere.

iCloud does all the syncing behind the scenes. iCloud combines the power of all the computers in Apple's cloud with programs running on each of your devices. Together they keep all your Apple devices synchronized with each other.

What kind of data does Apple sync between your devices?

Photos, Contacts, Mail, Calendars, Reminders, Pages, Numbers, Notes, Safari, News, and much more. iCloud constantly syncs all these different kinds of data between your devices.

As an example, if you have iCloud turned on and you take a photo on your phone, iCloud will sync that photo to all your devices. Look at your photo library on your iPad. The picture you took on your phone shows up there, soon after you took it.

All your photos (and other data) are securely stored in Apple's cloud. Even if you lose all your devices, you won't lose your photos. Apple tucks them safely away in their cloud. Get a new phone, log into your Apple account, and all your photos will magically appear.

Storing all your photos in the cloud lets Apple play a clever trick: you can take more photos than will fit on any of your devices (as long as you've paid for the cloud storage). How? Apple stores on each device the photos it thinks you are most likely to view. This will be different for each device because each device has different amounts of available storage. All your other photos are still up in the cloud. When you want to see a photo that's not on the device, Apple copies it to your device and removes some other photo to make room.

Comparing Apple to Google

Since Google is a major alternative to iCloud, it will help to understand how they differ. Google usually does not sync data between devices (though it can). Google Photos, which is Google's cloud service for managing photos, has every device access your photos directly from their cloud. No syncing needed. This is one reason why Google can make a version of their apps available on iOS, Android, and the web, while Apple apps work primarily on Apple devices.

Apple vs. Google Pros and Cons

How iCloud works is not wrong, or bad. It's just different and quite clever. However, there are pros and cons to Apple's cloud strategy.

The biggest con is getting the syncing right is extraordinarily complex, like rocket-science complex. In practice, this means there can be bugs in how the syncing works. Your data will be on one device and not on another, and you'll have no idea why or what to do about it.

The biggest pro is your data is available on your device. All your data is there, even without an internet connection, and accessing that data will be fast.

Should you use iCloud?

Once upon a time I would have said no. iCloud used to be buggy. It had lots of problems with data not syncing properly. Apple has ironed out most of those problems, so it's reliable enough to use now.

If you primarily use Apple devices, then iCloud is almost a no brainer. Yes, it's more expensive than it should be, but iCloud makes syncing painless so it's worth the cost. And if your family primarily uses Apple devices, it's a double no brainer, because there are a lot of cool features that allow families to share data with each other.

A huge downside of iCloud is that it only works on Apple devices. That's not completely true; some of the iCloud works on Windows, and over the web, but I wouldn't trust Apple's commitment to any non-Apple platform. Apple really wants to keep you in their ecosystem. Support for other platforms is likely to fall low on the priority list when it comes to fixing bugs and adding features.

If you use a mix of platforms, like Windows and Android, then iCloud may not be for you. You'll probably want to choose Google or a service from another vendor. A lot of people happily use Dropbox to sync files between all their devices, including Android and Windows devices. Dropbox, however, can't sync settings, photos, notes, contacts, and other data between iOS devices; only Apple can do that.

A huge advantage of iCloud is that it makes it easy to backup your iOS devices. We've talked about the importance of backing up your data many times. iCloud is one way you can do it. However, iCloud won't backup a laptop or desktop computer for you; you'll need to use another service like Carbonite.

You may find yourself using a mix of different services for different jobs. Use iCloud for your Apple devices. If you collaborate on documents with a group, Google Drive is often the way to go. And if you need to sync files between many kinds of different devices and share them with other people, then Dropbox is a popular option.

20

GOOGLE MAPS: A CLOUD SERVICE FOR NAVIGATION

I'm horrible with directions. So for me, the biggest use for my phone, is turn-by-turn navigation. It's a godsend. In fact, I programmed an iPhone app, called PicBak, to help me with directions.

Which app do I use for navigation? Google Maps. Apple Maps used to be horrible, and even though it's pretty good now, my default is good old trusty Google Maps. I have confidence Google Maps will always get me where I'm going.

Here's what Google Maps looks like:

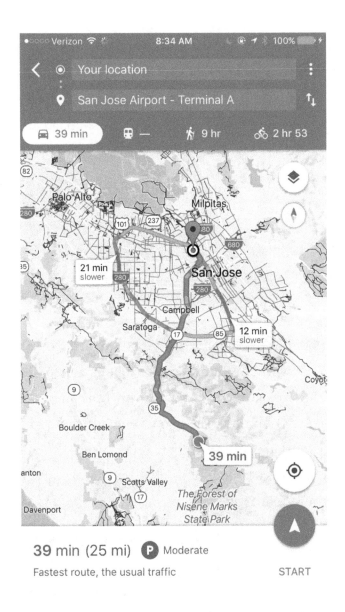

Press *Start* and Google Maps will talk you through getting from here to there. It calculates the fastest route given current and projected traffic patterns. If there's an accident, it reroutes you to the next best available route. You can look at how bad traffic is on any highway. If you want to compare routes, Google Maps will tell you how long each route will take. If you want to find the nearest coffee shop, it can tell you that too.

How does Google Maps accomplish all this deep magic? You guessed it, the cloud! Isn't the cloud cool?

To understand why the cloud is so important to Google Maps, let's think about how it would need to work if Google Maps worked only on your device.

The first point to consider is that Google Maps works everywhere in the world for hundreds of millions of people. Keep in mind the storage available on any device is limited. How could Google Maps have the maps for everywhere in the world on your device? It couldn't. That's way too much data. All those maps are stored in the cloud (as data) and downloaded (over the internet) as needed.

The next point to consider is where does Google Maps get all the traffic information for every place in the world? Is there a way for your device to know all the traffic information, for everyplace in the world? No, there's not. That information must come from other sources.

In the US, for example, Google gets a lot of traffic information from Verizon. Verizon is a cellular network provider, so they can tell when people are stuck in traffic by tracking the location of all those cell phones. Google also gets traffic reports from local departments of transportation. And, since a lot of people use Google Maps, Google Maps tells Google about local traffic conditions too.

In short, Google gets traffic information from a lot of different sources. Those sources will be different depending on where you are. In India, traffic information is available from different sources than it is in Iowa. Google must make software systems to collect data from all those different sources. Is that possible on your device? No, it's not. It's way too big and complicated a problem for your little phone to handle.

After Google takes in all the traffic data, a picture must be generated of what traffic looks like at any given time, in any given place. Could this happen on your device? Not a chance. It requires a huge amount of data. Your phone couldn't handle it.

Now let's consider route planning. You may not know this, but planning a route is a genuinely difficult problem to solve. If you are at one point on the map, there are thousands of different roads you could take to get to a different point on the map. The best route is selected by predicting future travel times on each route and picking the one taking the least time.

This requires a lot of information. Yes, it must know the current traffic conditions, but Google goes one step better. Google uses all the information they've collected over the years to predict likely traffic conditions, and they use their predictions when selecting a route. A lot of brainpower is needed to evaluate all those potential routes. Your phone can't do that.

The last thing we'll consider is Google Maps' ability to search for the nearest coffee shop. Google has to keep a giant points-of-interest map, so it knows about all the different things around you. Notice Google doesn't just show one coffee shop when you search for "best coffee shop." It gives you a list of shops and it also gives you a rating for each one, its hours of operation, how expensive it is, how far away you are from it now, and it will even show you a picture of what it looks like inside.

Here's an example of those search results:

How does Google know all that? Because Google keeps that kind of data for literally every place in the world. No way that fits on your phone.

So far it seems like your phone is useless in the whole process. Everything of interest happens in the cloud. Not at all. Consider this. How does Google Maps know where you are?

Your phone has a GPS feature (Global Positioning System). Using the GPS information from your phone, Google Maps continually reads your current location and sends it up to the cloud.

The Google Maps app on your phone is responsible for showing you the route, telling you the turn-by-turn directions, and reacting to any commands you give.

Google Maps will even store some data on your device so it can work for a little while without an internet connection.

Google Maps is **what a modern app looks like**. A lot happens in the cloud. You don't see it, but it's there, like an iceberg where 90% of the iceberg is underwater. Most of the heavy lifting is done in the cloud because the cloud has all the necessary resources to do the work.

But a lot happens on the phone too. If the internet connection goes down, Google Maps can't just stop working. That would be a disaster. An app needs enough data and enough smarts to do a lot of what the cloud does; only it must do it on the device. It's not easy to make that work.

There's a sophisticated dance of cooperation between a

device and the cloud that's quite beautiful when you think about it.

21

CLOUD DVR: TV IN THE CLOUD

Cloud DVRs are a good example of how a service can move from a local device to the cloud, and get a lot better in the process.

A DVR is a Digital Video Recorder. A DVR is a device connected to your TV that lets you record video to watch later. When you record a TV program, you're recording it on a DVR.

Here's a picture of our old DVR:

Yours probably looks similar. DVRs were an awesome invention. A DVR records a TV show so you can watch the show later, anytime you want. Such power! You don't need to be in front of a TV at a certain time anymore to watch a show. What an amazing freedom that is.

A DVR usually has a few standard features: it keeps a list of available shows for you to select from; it fast forwards past commercials (yeah!); it scrubs backward through video so a scene can be rewatched or be played in slow motion. A DVR may have lots of other features, but those are the basics.

A DVR usually has a few standard limitations as well: the number of simultaneous shows that can be recorded is limited by the number tuners, which means in practice only two shows can record at a time; the number of shows that can be stored on the DVR is limited. Once a DVR is full, old shows must be deleted to make room for new shows.

What do we know of that has unlimited space available? Oh yes, the cloud. So Cloud DVRs were invented.

YouTube TV, Sling TV, DirecTV Now, and Sony's Vue all are examples of services offering a Cloud DVR. A Cloud DVR is like the DVR that's attached to your TV, only it's in the cloud. You don't have a DVR box anymore. Instead, it's like any other cloud service we've described so far. You use an app to record and playback your shows.

Here's what my YouTube TV looks like:

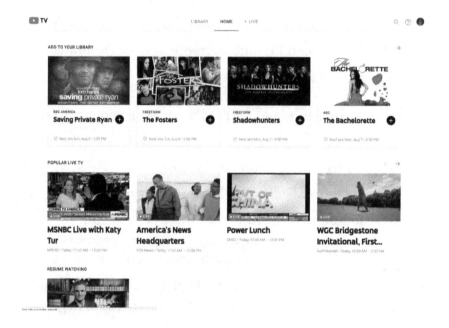

Searching for shows is like searching for anything else on Google. Select which shows you want to record and they'll record automatically.

And just like your old DVR, you can play a show back later, anytime you want, but there's a difference. YouTube TV lets you record six shows simultaneously, and there's no storage limit. You can store as much video as you want at no extra cost. And once you tell YouTube TV what your favorite show, league or team is, it will save all those games to your DVR, no matter on which channel they appear. Plus, you can watch those recordings on any device supporting YouTube TV, which is most everything.

Once again we see the benefits of moving to a cloud service.

The cloud service is smarter. The cloud has a massive amount of available resources. It learns what you like and automatically records shows it thinks you might want to watch later.

The cloud service has fewer limits. YouTube TV lets you record more video and keep more recordings.

The cloud service does more. YouTube TV can sort shows alphabetically, but you can also sort by *trending*, *top rated*, and *most popular*. Little features like this are easy to add to a cloud service.

The cloud service has a better user interface. DVR remotes and user interfaces are almost always slow, clunky, and difficult to use and understand.

The cloud service is easy to start using. Just sign up, and you can immediately start using YouTube TV.

The cloud service is easy to stop using. Tired of using YouTube TV? Cancel it. It's just that simple.

The cloud service doesn't have a physical device

that needs replacing when it breaks. The cloud service provider is responsible for all maintenance.

On the negative side, if you don't have a good internet connection, a Cloud DVR won't work for you at all. The internet giveth and the internet taketh away.

22

NETFLIX: WHAT HAPPENS WHEN YOU PRESS PLAY?

Netflix seems so simple. Press play and video magically appears. Easy, right? Not so much.

Given our discussion in the *What is Cloud Computing?* chapter, you might expect Netflix to serve video using AWS. Press play in a Netflix application and video stored in S3 would be streamed from S3, over the internet, directly to your device.

A completely sensible approach...for a much smaller service.

But that's not how Netflix works at all. It's far more complicated and interesting than you might imagine.

To see why let's look at some impressive Netflix statistics for 2017.

- Netflix has more than 110 million subscribers.
- Netflix operates in more than 200 countries.
- Netflix has nearly $3 billion in revenue per quarter.
- Netflix adds more than 5 million new subscribers per quarter.
- Netflix plays more than 1 billion hours of video each week. As a comparison, YouTube streams 1 billion hours of video *every day* while Facebook streams 110 million hours of video every day.
- Netflix played 250 million hours of video on a single day in 2017.
- Netflix accounts for over 37% of peak internet traffic in the United States.
- Netflix plans to spend $7 billion on new content in 2018.

What have we learned?

Netflix is huge. They're global, they have a lot of members, they play a lot of videos, and they have a lot of money.

Another relevant factoid is Netflix is subscription based. Members pay Netflix monthly and can cancel at any time. When you press play to chill on Netflix, it had better work. Unhappy members unsubscribe.

We're Going Deep

Netflix is a terrific example of all the ideas we've talked about, which is why this chapter goes into a lot more detail than the other cloud services we've covered.

One big reason for diving deeper into Netflix is they make much more information available than other companies.

Netflix holds *communication* as a central cultural value. Netflix more than lives up to its standards.

In fact, I'd like to thank Netflix for being so open about their architecture. Over the years, Netflix has given hundreds of talks and written hundreds of articles on the inner-workings of how they operate. The whole industry is better for it.

Another reason for going into so much detail on Netflix is Netflix is just plain fascinating. Most of us have used Netflix at one time or another. Who wouldn't love peeking behind the curtain to see what makes Netflix tick?

Netflix operates in two clouds: AWS and Open Connect.

How does Netflix keep their members happy? With the cloud of course. Actually, Netflix uses two different clouds: AWS and Open Connect.

Both clouds must work together seamlessly to deliver endless hours of customer-pleasing video.

The three parts of Netflix: client, backend, content delivery network (CDN).

You can think of Netflix as being divided into three parts: the client, the backend, and the content delivery network (CDN).

The *client* is the user interface on any device used to browse and play Netflix videos. It could be an app on your iPhone, a website on your desktop computer, or even an app on your Smart TV. Netflix controls each and every client for each and every device.

Everything that happens before you hit *play* happens in the *backend*, which runs in AWS. That includes things like preparing all new incoming video and handling requests from all apps, websites, TVs, and other devices.

Everything that happens after you hit *play* is handled by

Open Connect. Open Connect is Netflix's custom global content delivery network (CDN). Open Connect stores Netflix video in different locations throughout the world. When you press play the video streams from Open Connect, into your device, and is displayed by the client. Don't worry; we'll talk more about what a CDN is a little later.

Interestingly, at Netflix they don't actually say *hit play on video*, they say *clicking start on a title*. Every industry has its own lingo.

By controlling all three areas—client, backend, CDN— Netflix has achieved complete vertical integration.

Netflix controls your video viewing experience from beginning to end. That's why it just works when you click play from anywhere in the world. You reliably get the content you want to watch when you want to watch it.

Let's see how Netflix makes that happen.

In 2008 Netflix Started Moving to AWS

Netflix launched in 1998. At first they rented DVDs through the US Postal Service. But Netflix saw the future was on-demand streaming video.

In 2007 Netflix introduced their streaming video-on-demand

service that allowed subscribers to stream television series and films via the Netflix website on personal computers, or the Netflix software on a variety of supported platforms, including smartphones and tablets, digital media players, video game consoles, and smart TVs.

On a personal note, that streaming video-on-demand was the future might seem obvious. And it was. I worked at a couple of startups that tried to make a video-on-demand product. They failed.

Netflix succeeded. Netflix certainly executed well, but they were late to the game, and that helped them. By 2007 the internet was fast enough and cheap enough to support streaming video services. That was never the case before. The addition of fast, low-cost mobile bandwidth and the introduction of powerful mobile devices like smart phones and tablets, has made it easier and cheaper for anyone to stream video at any time from anywhere. Timing is everything.

Netflix Began by Running their Own Datacenters

EC2 was just getting started in 2007, about the same time Netflix's streaming service started. There was no way Netflix could have launched using EC2.

Netflix built two datacenters, located right next to each other.

They experienced all the problems we talked about in earlier chapters.

Building out a datacenter is a lot of work. Ordering equipment takes a long time. Installing and getting all the equipment working takes a long time. And as soon they got everything working they would run out of capacity, and the whole process had to start over again.

The long lead times for equipment forced Netflix to adopt what is known as a *vertical scaling* strategy. Netflix made big programs that ran on big computers. This approach is called building a *monolith*. One program did everything.

The problem is when you're growing really fast like Netflix; it's very hard to make a monolith reliable. And it wasn't.

A Service Outage Caused Netflix to Move to AWS

For three days in August 2008, Netflix could not ship DVDs because of corruption in their database. This was unacceptable. Netflix had to do something.

The experience of building datacenters had taught Netflix an important lesson—they weren't good at building datacenters.

What Netflix was good at was delivering video to their members. Netflix would rather concentrate on getting better at delivering video rather than getting better at building data-centers. Building datacenters was not a competitive advantage for Netflix, delivering video is.

At that time, Netflix decided to move to AWS. AWS was just getting established, so selecting AWS was a bold move.

Netflix moved to AWS because it wanted a more reliable infrastructure. Netflix wanted to remove any single point of failure from its system. AWS offered highly reliable databases, storage and redundant datacenters. Netflix wanted cloud computing, so it wouldn't have to build big unreliable monoliths anymore. Netflix wanted to become a global service without building its own datacenters. None of these capabilities were available in its old datacenters and never would be.

A reason Netflix gave for choosing AWS was it didn't want to do any *undifferentiated heavy lifting*. Undifferentiated heavy lifting are those things that have to be done, but don't provide any advantage to the core business of providing a quality video watching experience. AWS does all the undifferentiated heavy lifting for Netflix. This lets Netflixians focus on providing business value.

It took more than eight years for Netflix to complete the process of moving from their own datacenters to AWS. During that period Netflix grew its number of streaming customers eightfold. Netflix now runs on several hundred thousand EC2 instances.

Netflix is More Reliable in AWS

It's not like Netflix has never experienced down time on AWS, but on the whole, its service is much more reliable than it was before.

You don't see complaints like this very often anymore:

or this:

Netflix is so reliable now because they've taken extraordinary steps to make their service reliable.

Netflix operates out of three AWS regions: one in North Virginia, one in Portland Oregon, and one in Dublin Ireland.

Within each region, Netflix operates in three different availability zones.

Netflix has said there are no plans to operate out of more regions. It's very expensive and complicated to add new regions. Most companies operate out of just one region, let alone two or three.

The advantage of having three regions is that any one region can fail, and the other regions will step in handle all the members in the failed region. When a region fails, Netflix calls this *evacuating* a region.

Let's use an example. Let's say you're watching a new *House of Cards* episode in London England. Because it's closest to London, chances are your Netflix device is connected to the Dublin region.

What happens if the entire Dublin region fails? Does that mean Netflix should stop working for you? Of course not!

Netflix, after detecting the failure, redirects you to Virginia. Your device would now talk to the Virginia region instead of Dublin. You might not even notice there was a failure.

How often does an AWS region fail? Once a month. Well, a region doesn't actually fail every month. Netflix runs monthly tests. Every month Netflix causes a region to fail on purpose just to make sure its system can handle region level failures. A region can be evacuated in six minutes.

Netflix calls this their *global services model*. Any customer can be served out of any region. This is amazing. And it doesn't happen automatically. AWS has no magic sauce for handling region failures or serving customers out of multiple regions. Netflix has done all this work on its own. Netflix is a pioneer in figuring out how to create reliable systems using multiple regions. I'm not aware of any other company that goes to these lengths to make their service so reliable.

Another advantage of being in these three regions is that it gives Netflix world-wide coverage. Netflix ran some tests and found if you use a Netflix application anywhere in the world, you'll get fast service from one of these three regions.

Netflix Saves Money in AWS

This may surprise a lot of people, but AWS is cheaper for Netflix. The cloud costs per streaming view ended up being a fraction of the cost of its old datacenters.

Why? The elasticity of the cloud.

Netflix could add servers when it needed them and return them when it didn't. Rather than have a lot of extra computers hanging around doing nothing just to handle peak load, Netflix only had to pay for what was needed, when it was needed.

All the stuff we talked about in the *What is Cloud Computing?* chapter.

What Happens in AWS Before you Press Play?

Anything that doesn't involve serving video is handled in AWS.

This includes scalable computing, scalable storage, business logic, scalable distributed databases, big data processing and analytics, recommendations, transcoding, and hundreds of other functions.

Don't worry, you don't need to understand what all those things are, but since you may find it interesting, I'll explain them briefly.

Scalable computing and scalable storage.

Scalable computing is EC2 and *scalable storage* is S3. Nothing new for us here.

Your Netflix device—iPhone, TV, Xbox, Android phone, tablet, etc.—talks to a Netflix service running in EC2.

View a list of potential videos to watch? That's your Netflix device contacting a computer in EC2 to get the list.

Ask for more details about a video? That's your Netflix device contacting a computer in EC2 to get the details.

It's just like all the other cloud services we've talked about in the book.

Scalable distributed database.

Netflix uses both DynamoDB and Cassandra for their distributed databases. Not that these names should mean anything to you, they're just high-quality database products.

Database. A database stores data. Your profile information, your billing information, all the movies you've ever watched, all that kind of information is stored in a database.

Distributed. Distributed means the database doesn't run on one big computer, it runs on many computers. Your data is copied to multiple computers so if one or even two computers holding your data fail, your data will be safe. In fact, your data is copied to all three regions. That way, if a region fails your data will be there when the new region is ready to start using it.

Scalable. Scalable means the database can handle as much data as you ever want to put into it. That's one major advantage of being a distributed database. More computers can be added as necessary to handle more data.

Big data processing and analytics.

Big data simply means there's a lot of data. Netflix collects a lot of information. Netflix knows what everyone has watched when they watched it and where they were when they watched. Netflix knows which videos members have looked at but decided not to watch. Netflix knows how many times each video has been watched...and a lot more.

Putting all the data in a standard format is called *processing*.

Making sense of all that data is called *analytics*. Data is analyzed to answer specific questions.

Netflix personalizes artwork just for you.

Here's a great example of how Netflix entices you to watch more videos using its data analytics capabilities.

When browsing around looking for something to watch on Netflix, have you noticed there's always an image displayed for each video? That's called the *header image*.

The header image is meant to intrigue you, to draw you into selecting a video. The idea is the more compelling the header image, the more likely you are to watch a video. And the more videos you watch, the less likely you are to unsubscribe from Netflix.

Here's an example of different header images for *Stranger Things*:

Netflix

You might be surprised to learn the image shown for each video is selected specifically for you. Not everyone sees the same image.

Everyone used to see the same header image. Here's how it worked. Members were shown at a random one picture from a group of options, like the pictures in the above *Stranger Things* collage. Netflix counted every time a video was watched, recording which picture was displayed when the video was selected.

For our *Stranger Things* example, let's say when the group picture in the center was shown, *Stranger Things* was watched 1,000 times. For all the other pictures, it was watched only once each.

Since the group picture was the best at getting members to watch, Netflix would make it the header image for *Stranger Things* forever.

This is called being *data-driven*. Netflix is known for being a data-driven company. Data is gathered—in this case, the number of views associated with each picture—and used to make the best decisions possible—in this case, which header image to select.

Clever, but can you imagine doing better? Yes, by using more data. That's the theme of the future—solving problems by learning from data.

You and I are likely very different people. Do you think we are motivated by the same kind of header image? Probably not. We have different tastes. We have different preferences.

Netflix knows this too. That's why Netflix personalizes all the images they show you. Netflix tries to select the artwork highlighting the most relevant aspect of a video to you. How do they do that?

Remember, Netflix records and counts everything you do on their site. They know which kind of movies you like best, which actors you like the most, and so on.

Let's say one of your recommendations is the movie *Good Will Hunting*. Netflix must choose a header image to show you. The goal is to show an image that lets you know about a movie you'll probably be interested in. Which image should Netflix show you?

If you like comedies, Netflix will show you an image featuring Robin Williams. If you prefer romantic movies, Netflix will show you an image Matt Damon and Minnie Driver poised for a kiss.

Netflix

By showing Robin Williams, Netflix is letting you know there's likely to be humor in the movie and because Netflix knows you like comedies, this video is a good match.

The Matt Damon and Minnie Driver image conveys a completely different message. If you're a comedy fan and saw this image, you might skip right on by.

That's why selecting the right header image is so important. It sends a strong personalized signal indicating what a movie is about.

Here's another example, *Pulp Fiction.*

Netflix

If you've watched a lot of movies starring Uma Thurman, then you're likely to see the header image featuring Uma. If you've watched a lot of movies starring John Travolta, then you're likely to see the header image featuring John.

Can you see how choosing the best possible personalized artwork might make you more likely to watch a video?

Netflix appeals to your interests when selecting artwork, yet Netflix doesn't want to lie to you either. They don't want to show a clickbait image just to get you to watch a video you may not like. There's no incentive in that. Netflix isn't paid per video watched. Netflix tries to *minimize regret*. Netflix wants you to be happy with the videos you watch, so they pick the best header images they can.

This is just one small example of how data analysis is used by Netflix. Netflix uses these kind of strategies everywhere.

Recommendations.

Usually Netflix will show you only 40 to 50 video options, yet they have many thousands of videos available.

How does Netflix decide? Using machine learning.

That's part of the *big data processing and analytics* we just talked about. Netflix looks at its data and predicts what you'll like. Nobody else's Netflix screen looks like yours. Everything you see see on a Netflix screen is chosen specifically for you using machine learning.

Transcoding From Source Media to What You Watch

Here's where we start transitioning into how video is handled by Netflix.

Before you can watch a video on your favorite device of choice, Netflix must convert the video into a format that works best for your device. This process is called *transcoding* or *encoding*.

Transcoding is the process that converts a video file from one format to another, to make videos viewable across different platforms and devices.

Netflix encodes all its video in AWS on as many as 300,000 CPUs at one time. That's larger than most super computers!

The source of source media.

Who sends video to Netflix? Production houses and studios. Netflix calls this video *source media*. The new video is given to the *Content Operations Team* for processing.

The video comes in a high definition format that's many terabytes in size. A terabyte is big. Imagine 60 stacks of paper as tall as the Eiffel Tower. That's a terabyte.

Before you can view a video, Netflix puts it through a rigorous multi-step process.

Netflix

Validating the video.

The first thing Netflix does is spend a lot of time validating the video. It looks for digital artifacts, color changes, or missing frames that may have been caused by previous transcoding attempts or data transmission problems.

The video is rejected if any problems are found.

Into the media pipeline.

After the video is validated, it's fed into what Netflix calls the *media pipeline*.

A *pipeline* is simply a series of steps data is put through to make it ready for use, much like an assembly line in a factory. More than 70 different pieces of software have a hand in creating every video.

It's not practical to process a single multi-terabyte sized file, so the first step of the pipeline is to break the video into lots of smaller chunks.

The video chunks are then put through the pipeline so they can be encoded *in parallel*. In parallel simply means the chunks are processed at the same time.

Let's illustrate parallelism with an example.

Let's say you have one hundred dirty dogs that need washing. Which would be faster, one person washing the dogs one after another? Or would it be faster to hire one hundred dog washers and wash them all the same time?

Obviously, it's faster to have one hundred dog washers working at the same time. That's parallelism. And that's why Netflix uses so many servers in EC2. They need a lot of servers to process these huge video files in parallel. It works too. Netflix says a source media file can be encoded and pushed to their CDN in as little as 30 minutes.

Once the chunks are encoded, they're validated to make sure no new problems have been introduced.

Then the chunks are assembled back into a file and validated once again.

The result is a pile of files.

The encoding process creates a lot of files. Why? The end goal for Netflix is to support every internet-connected device.

Netflix started streaming video in 2007 on Microsoft Windows. Over time more devices were added—Roku, LG, Samsung Blu-ray, Apple Mac, Xbox 360, LG DTV, Sony PS3, Nintendo Wii, Apple iPad, Apple iPhone, Apple TV, Android, Kindle Fire, and Comcast X1.

In all, Netflix supports 2200 different devices. Each device has a video format that looks best on that particular device. If you're watching Netflix on an iPhone, you'll see a video that gives you the best viewing experience on the iPhone.

Netflix calls all the different formats for a video its *encoding profile*.

Netflix also creates files optimized for different network speeds. If you're watching on a fast network, you'll see higher quality video than you would if you're watching over a slow network.

There are also files for different audio formats. Audio is encoded into different levels of quality and in different languages.

There are also files included for subtitles. A video may have subtitles in a number of different languages.

There are a lot of different viewing options for every video. What you see depends on your device, your network quality, your Netflix plan, and your language choice.

Just how many files are we talking about?

For *The Crown*, Netflix stores around 1,200 files!

Stranger Things season 2 has even more files. It was shot in 8K and has nine episodes. The source video files were many, many terabytes of data. It took 190,000 CPU hours to encode just one season.

The result? 9,570 different video, audio, and text files!

Let's see how Netflix plays all that video.

Three Different Strategies for Streaming Video

Netflix has tried three different video streaming strategies its own small CDN; third-party CDNs; and Open Connect.

Let's start by defining CDN. A CDN is a *content distribution network*.

Content for Netflix—is of course—the video files we discussed in the previous section.

Distribution means video files are copied from a central location, over a *network* and stored on computers located all over the world.

For Netflix, the central location where videos are stored is S3.

Why build a CDN?

The idea behind a CDN is simple: put video as close as possible to users by spreading computers throughout the world. When a user wants to watch a video, find the nearest computer with the video on it and stream to the device from there.

The biggest benefits of a CDN are speed and reliability.

Imagine you're watching a video in London and the video is being streamed from Portland, Oregon. The video stream must pass through a lot of networks, including an undersea cable, so the connection will be slow and unreliable.

By moving video content as close as possible to the people watching it, the viewing experience will be as fast and reliable as possible.

Each location with a computer storing video content is called a PoP or *point of presence*. Each PoP is a physical location that provides access to the internet. It houses servers, routers, and other telecommunications equipment. We'll talk more about PoPs later.

The First CDN Was Too Small

In 2007, when Netflix debuted its new streaming service, it had 36 million members in 50 countries, watching more than a billion hours of video each month, streaming multiple terabits of content per second.

To support the streaming service, Netflix built its own simple CDN in five different locations within the United States.

The Netflix video catalog was small enough at the time that each location contained all of its content.

The Second CDNs Were Too Big

In 2009, Netflix decided to use 3rd-party CDNs. Around this time, the pricing for 3rd-party CDNs was coming down.

Using 3rd-party CDNs made perfect sense for Netflix. Why spend all the time and effort building a CDN of your own when you can instantly reach the globe using existing CDN services?

Netflix contracted with companies like Akamai, Limelight, and Level 3 to provide CDN services. There's nothing wrong with using third-party CDNs. In fact, pretty much every company does. For example, the NFL has used Akamai to stream live football games.

By not building out its own CDN, Netflix had more time to work on other higher priority projects.

Netflix put a lot of time and effort into developing smarter clients. Netflix created algorithms to adapt to changing networks conditions. Even in the face of errors, overloaded networks, and overloaded servers, Netflix wants members always viewing the best picture possible. One technique Netflix developed is switching to a different video source— say another CDN, or a different server—to get a better result.

At the same time, Netflix was also devoting a lot of effort into all the AWS services we talked about earlier. Netflix calls the services in AWS its *control plane*. Control plane is a telecommunications term identifying the part of the system that controls everything else. In your body, your brain is the control plane; it controls everything else.

Then Netflix thought it could do better by developing it's own CDN.

Open Connect Was Just Right

In 2011, Netflix realized at its scale it needed a dedicated CDN solution to maximize network efficiency. Video distribution is a core competency for Netflix and could be a huge competitive advantage.

So Netflix started developing Open Connect, its own purpose-built CDN. Open Connect launched in 2012.

Open Connect has a lot of advantages for Netflix:

- *Less expensive.* 3rd-party CDNs are expensive. Doing it themselves would save a lot of money.
- *Better quality.* By controlling the entire video path—transcoding, CDN, clients on devices—Netflix reasoned it could deliver a superior video viewing experience.

- *More Scalable.* Netflix has the goal of providing service everywhere in the world. Quickly supporting all those people while providing a quality video viewing experience required building its own system.

The 3rd-party CDNs must support users accessing any kind of content from anywhere in the world. Netflix has a much simpler job.

Netflix knows exactly who its users are because they must subscribe to Netflix. Netflix knows exactly which videos it needs to serve. Just knowing it only has to serve large video streams allows Netflix to make a lot of smart optimization choices other CDNs can't make. Netflix also knows a lot about it members. The company knows which videos they like to watch and when they like to watch them.

With this kind of knowledge, Netflix built a really high-performing CDN. Let's go into more details on how Open Connect works.

Open Connect Appliances

Remember how we said a CDN has computers distributed all over the world?

Netflix developed its own computer system for video storage. Netflix calls them Open Connect Appliances or OCAs.

Here's what an early OCA installation in a site looked like:

Netflix

There are many OCAs in the above picture. OCAs are grouped into clusters of multiple servers.

Each OCA is a fast server, highly optimized for delivering large files, with lots and lots of hard disks or flash drives for storing video.

Here's what one of the OCA servers looks like:

Open Connect Appliance - Global

Netflix

There are several different kinds of OCAs for different purposes. There are large OCAs that can store Netflix's entire video catalog. There are smaller OCAs that can store only a portion of Netflix's video catalog. Smaller OCAs are filled with video every day, during off-peak hours, using a process Netflix calls *proactive caching*. We'll talk more about how proactive caching works later.

From a hardware perspective, there's nothing special about OCAs. They're based on commodity PC components and assembled in custom cases by various suppliers. You could buy the same computers if you wanted to.

Notice how all Netflix's computers are red? Netflix had their computers specially made to match their logo color.

From a software perspective, OCAs use the FreeBSD operating system and NGINX for the web server. Yes, every OCA has a web server. Video streams using NGINX. If none of these names make any sense, don't worry, I'm just including them for completeness.

The number of OCAs on a site depends on how reliable Netflix wants the site to be, the amount of Netflix traffic (bandwidth) that is delivered from that site, and the percentage of traffic a site allows to be streamed.

When you press play, you're watching video streaming from a specific OCA, like the one above, in a location near you.

For the best possible video viewing experience, what Netflix would really like to do is cache video in your house. But that's not practical yet. The next best thing is to put a mini-Netflix as close to your house as they can. How do they do that?

Where does Netflix put Open Connect Appliances (OCAs)?

Netflix delivers huge amounts of video traffic from thousands of servers in more than 1,000 locations around the world. Take a look at this map of video serving locations:

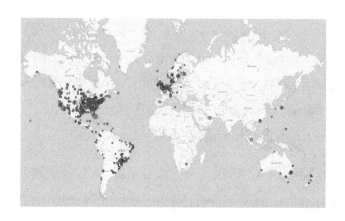

Netflix

Other video services, like YouTube and Amazon, deliver video on their own backbone network. These companies literally built their own global network for delivering video to users. That's very complicated and very expensive to do.

Netflix took a completely different approach to building its CDN.

Netflix doesn't operate its own network; it doesn't operate its own datacenters anymore either. Instead, internet service providers (ISPs) agree to put OCAs in their datacenters. OCAs are offered free to ISPs to embed in their networks. Netflix also puts OCAs in or close to internet exchange locations (IXPs).

Using this strategy Netflix doesn't need to operate its own datacenters, yet it gets all the benefits of being in a regular datacenter it's just someone else's datacenter. Genius!

Those last two paragraphs were pretty dense, so let's break it down.

Using ISPs to build a CDN.

An ISP is your internet provider. It's who you get your internet service from. It might be Verizon, Comcast, or thousands of other services.

The main point here is ISPs are located all around the world and they're close to customers. By placing OCAs in ISP datacenters, Netflix is also all over the world, and close to its customers.

Using IXPs to build a CDN.

An internet exchange location is a datacenter where ISPs and CDNs exchange internet traffic between their networks. It's just like going to a party to exchange Christmas presents with your friends. It's easier to exchange presents if everyone is in one place. It's easier to exchange network traffic if everyone is one place.

IXPs are located all over the world:

TeleGeography's Internet Exchange Map

Here's what the London Internet Exchange looks like:

London Internet Exchange (LINX)

Drill down on those yellow fiber optic cables and what you'll see is something like this from the AMS-IX Internet exchange point, in Amsterdam, Netherlands:

Each wire in the above picture connects one network to another network. That's how different networks exchange traffic with each other.

An IXP is like a highway interchange, only using wires:

For Netflix, this is another win. IXPs are all over the world. So by putting their OCAs in IXPs, Netflix doesn't have to run its own datacenters.

Video is Proactively Cached to OCAs Every Day

Netflix has all this video sitting in S3. They have all these video serving computers spread throughout the world. There's just one thing missing: Video!

Netflix uses a process it calls *proactive caching* to efficiently copy video to OCAs.

What is a cache?

A cache is a hiding place, especially one in the ground, for ammunition, food and treasures.

You know how squirrels bury nuts for the winter?

Each location they bury nuts is a *cache*. During the winter, any squirrel can find a nut cache and chow down.

Arctic explorers sent small teams ahead to cache food, fuel and other supplies along the route they were taking. The larger team following behind would stop at every cache location and resupply.

Both the squirrels and Arctic explorers were being *proactive*; they were doing something ahead of time to prepare for later.

Each OCA is a video cache of what you'll most likely want to watch.

Netflix caches video by predicting what you'll want to watch.

Everywhere in the world, Netflix, knows to a high degree of accuracy what its members like to watch and when they like to watch it. Remember how we said Netflix was a data-driven company?

Netflix uses its popularity data to *predict* which videos members probably will want to watch tomorrow in each location. Here, *location* means a cluster of OCAs housed within an ISP or IXP.

Netflix copies the predicted videos to one or more OCAs at each location. This is called *prepositioning*. Video is placed on OCAs before anyone even asks.

This gives great service to members. The video they want to watch is already close to them, ready and available for streaming.

Netflix operates what is called a *tiered caching system.*

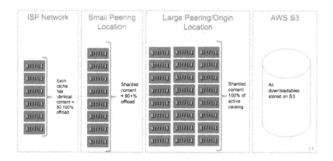

Netflix

The smaller OCAs we talked about earlier are placed in ISPs and IXPs. These are too small to contain the entire Netflix catalog of videos. Other locations have OCAs containing most of Netflix's video catalog. Still, other locations have big OCAs containing the entire Netflix catalog. These get their videos from S3.

Every night, each OCA wakes up and asks a service in AWS which videos it should have. The service in AWS sends the OCA a list of videos it's supposed to have based on the predictions we talked about earlier.

Each OCA is in charge of making sure it has all the videos on its list. If an OCA in the same location has one of the videos it's supposed to have, then it will copy the video from the local OCA. Otherwise, a nearby OCA with the video will be found and copied.

Since Netflix forecasts what will be popular tomorrow, there's always a one day lead time before a video is required to be on an OCA. This means videos can be copied during quiet, off-peak hours, substantially reducing bandwidth usage for ISPs.

There's never a *cache miss* in Open Connect. A cache miss would be asking for a specific video from an OCA and the OCA saying it doesn't have it. Cache misses happen all the time on other CDNs because you can't afford to copy content everywhere. Since Netflix knows all the videos it must cache, it knows exactly where each video is at all times. If a smaller OCA doesn't have a video, then one of the larger OCAs is always guaranteed to have it.

Why doesn't Netflix just copy all their video to every OCA in the world? Its video catalog is way too large to store everything at all locations. In 2013, the video catalog for Netflix was over 3 petabytes; I have no idea how large it is today, but I can only assume it's significantly larger.

That's why Netflix developed the method of choosing which videos to store on each OCA using data to *predict* what their members will want to watch.

Let's take an example. *House of Cards* is a very popular show. Which OCAs should it be copied to? Probably every location because members worldwide will want to watch House of Cards.

What if a video isn't as popular as House of Cards? Netflix decides which locations it should be copied to in order to best serve nearby member requests.

Within a location, a popular video like House of Cards is copied to many different OCAs. The more popular a video, the more servers it will be copied to. Why? If there was only one copy of a very popular video, streaming the video to members would overwhelm the server. As they say, many hands make light work.

A video isn't considered live when it's copied to just one OCA. Netflix wants to be able to play the same content at the same time everywhere in the world. Only when there are a sufficient number of OCAs with enough copies of the video to serve it appropriately, will the video be considered live and ready for members to watch.

Daredevil Season 2 in 2016, for example, was the first time Netflix released all episodes of a show, on all devices, in all countries, at the same time.

Hosting OCAs: What's in it for ISPs?

Why would an ISP agree to put an OCA cluster inside their network? At first blush, it seems too generous, but you'll be happy to know it's rooted firmly in self-interest.

To understand why, we'll need to talk about how networks work. I know throughout this book we've said cloud services are accessed over the internet. That's not the case for Netflix, at least when watching a video. When using a Netflix app, it talks to AWS over the internet.

The internet is an interconnect of networks. You have an ISP that provides internet service. I get my internet service from Comcast. What that means is my house connects to Comcast's network using a fiber optic cable. Comcast's network is their network; it's not the internet, the internet is something else.

Let's say I want to do a Google search, and I type a query into my browser and hit enter.

My request to Google first flows over Comcast's network. Google isn't on Comcast's network. At some point, my request has to go to Google's network. That's what the internet is for.

The internet connects Comcast's network to Google's network. There are these things called *routing protocols* that act like a traffic cop, directing where network traffic goes.

When my Google query is routed onto the internet it's not on Comcast's network anymore, and it's not on Google's network. It's on what's called the *internet backbone*.

The internet is woven together from many privately owned networks that choose to interoperate with each other. The IXPs we looked at earlier are one way networks connect with each other.

In the United States, here's a map of the long haul fiber network:

InterTubes: A Study of the US Long-haul Fiber-optic Infrastructure

What Netflix has done with Open Connect is placed its OCA clusters inside the ISPs network. That means if I watch a Netflix video I'll be talking to an OCA in Comcast's network. All my video traffic is on Comcast's network; it never hits the internet.

The key to scaling video delivery is to be as close to users as possible. When you're doing that you're not using the internet backbone. Requests are being satisfied on a local part of the network.

Why is this a good thing? Recall that we said Netflix already consumes more than 37% of the internet traffic in the United

States. If ISPs didn't cooperate, Netflix would use even more of the internet. The internet couldn't handle all the video traffic. ISPs would have to add a lot more network capacity, and that's expensive to build.

Right now, up to 100% of Netflix content is being served from within ISP networks. This reduces costs by relieving internet congestion for ISPs. At the same time, Netflix members experience a high-quality viewing experience. And network performance improves for everyone.

It's a win-win.

Open Connect is Reliable and Resilient

Earlier we discussed how Netflix increased the reliability of its system by running out of three different AWS regions. The architecture of Open Connect accomplished the same goal.

What may not be immediately obvious is that the OCAs are independent of each other. OCAs act as self-sufficient video-serving archipelagos. Members streaming from one OCA are not affected when other OCAs fail.

What happens when an OCA fails? The Netflix client you're using immediately switches to another OCA and resumes streaming.

What happens if too many people in one location use an OCA? The Netflix client will find a more lightly loaded OCA to use.

What happens if the network a member is using to stream video becomes overloaded? The same sort of thing. The Netflix client will find another OCA on a better performing network.

Open Connect is a very reliable and resilient system.

Netflix Controls the Client

Netflix handles failures gracefully because it controls the client on every device running Netflix.

Netflix develops its Android and iOS apps themselves, so you might expect them to control those. But even on platforms like Smart TVs, where Netflix doesn't build the client, Netflix still has control because it controls the *software development kit* (SDK).

A SDK is *a set of software development tools that allows the creation of applications.* Every Netflix app makes requests to AWS and plays video using the SDK.

By controlling the SDK, Netflix can adapt consistently and transparently to slow networks, failed OCAs, and any other problems that might arise.

Finally: Here's What Happens when You Press Play

It's been a long road getting here. We've learned a lot. Here's what we've learned so far:

- Netflix can be divided into three parts: the backend, the client, and the CDN.
- All requests from Netflix clients are handled in AWS.
- All video is streamed from a nearby Open Connect Appliance (OCA) in the Open Connect CDN.
- Netflix operates out of three AWS regions and can usually handle a failure in any region without members even noticing.
- New video content is transformed by Netflix into many different formats so the best format can be selected for viewing based on the device type, network quality, geographic location, and the member's subscription plan.
- Every day, over Open Connect, Netflix distributes video throughout the world, based on what they predict members in each location will want to watch.

Here's a picture of how Netflix describes the play process:

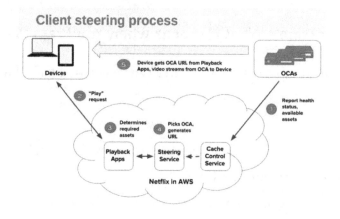

Netflix

Now, let's complete the picture:

- You select a video to watch using a client running on some device. The client sends a *play* request, indicating which video you want to play, to Netflix's *Playback Apps* service running in AWS.
- We've not talked about this before, but a big part of what happens after you hit play has to do with licensing. Not every location in the world has a license to view every video. Netflix must determine if you have a valid license to view a particular video. We won't talk about how that works—it's really boring—but keep in mind it's always happening. One reason Netflix started developing its own content is to avoid licensing issues. Netflix wants to release a show to everyone in the world all at the

same time. Creating its own content is the easiest way for Netflix to avoid worrying about licensing problems.

- Taking into account all the relevant information, the Playback Apps service returns URLs for up to ten different OCA servers. These are the same sort of URLs you use all the time in your web browser. Netflix uses your IP address and information from ISPs to identify which OCA clusters are best for you to use.

- The client intelligently selects which OCA to use. It does this by testing the quality of the network connection to each OCA. It will connect to the fastest, most reliable OCA first. The client keeps running these tests throughout the video streaming process.

- The client probes to figure out the best way to receive content from the OCA.

- The client connects to the OCA and starts streaming video to your device.

- Have you noticed when watching a video the picture quality varies? Sometimes it will look pixelated, and after awhile the picture snaps back to HD quality? That's because the client is adapting to the quality of the network. If the network quality declines, the client lowers video quality to match.

The client will switch to another OCA when the quality declines too much.

That's what happens when you press play on Netflix. Who would have ever thought so simple a thing as watching a video was so complex?

23

FIGHTING THE ECOSYSTEM WARS IN
THE PROACTIVE CLOUD

**The cloud is always busy proactively
working for you in the background. That's
how cloud services compete with each
other to keep you in their ecosystem.**

Most of the cloud services we've talked about so far have been request driven. You initiate a request and the cloud does something for you. You read a book. You search for the nearest coffee shop. You navigate to a destination. You send a message. You play a movie.

Handling direct requests is not all a cloud is good for. In fact, the biggest potential of the cloud is how it can proactively perform jobs for you in the background, without you asking or even knowing that it can be done.

Let's set this up:

- The cloud has a lot of compute power.
- The cloud has all your data.
- The cloud has access to a lot of other data in the world.
- Cloud providers have a lot of very smart programmers.
- As a cloud customer, you represent a very valuable recurring revenue stream.
- To keep your business and keep you within their ecosystem, cloud companies want to continually surprise and delight you.

How does a cloud company surprise and delight you?

- *By adding new features.* The more features you use, the more likely you'll stay in their ecosystem of services.
- *By inventing really clever products* that can only be done with a lot of compute power, a lot of data, and a lot of smart programmers.

Competition is driving the cloud to become *proactive.* Proactive means *taking action to control a situation rather than just responding to it after it has happened.*

What kind of actions? Those are the clever features and inventions, we'll talk more about these in a moment.

The key point to understand is: **the list of jobs cloud services will perform for you will only grow. And grow. And grow. And grow.**

Why? We are in the middle of the ecosystem wars. Google, Apple, Amazon, Facebook, and anyone else brave enough to play in the cloud space, want you to keep using their services and only their services.

The more valuable features they add, the greater the gravitational attraction to their service.

What do I mean by ecosystem?

An ecosystem—from a software perspective—is a community of interacting services in a single provider's environment.

I'll illustrate using a personal example. When Amazon released their Echo product, I bought it immediately.

If you don't already know, Amazon Echo is *a hands-free speaker you control with your voice. Echo connects to the Alexa Voice Service to play music, make calls, send and receive messages, provide information, news, sports scores, weather, and more—instantly. All you have to do is ask.*

It's like Apple's Siri; only you don't need your phone to use it. Our Echo sits on our kitchen counter.

We mostly use Echo to play music, listen to radio stations, set timers when cooking, ask about the weather, and occasionally ask general questions.

To talk to an Echo, you lead with the keyword *Alexa* and then speak a command. It's just how you would talk to Siri.

Here are some example Alexa commands:

- Alexa, set timer for 5 minutes

- Alexa, increase volume
- Alexa, give me my Flash Briefing
- Alexa, what's on my calendar for today?
- Alexa, turn on the lights
- Alexa, order walnuts

There are thousands more. Let's go through an example in more detail. The example should feel familiar because Alexa is a cloud service and works like all the cloud services we've talked about. The difference is instead of using an app or a web page, you talk to a device that sits on a nearby table.

Let's say I'm standing in my kitchen and say, "Alexa, play Etta James."

The Echo is listening all the time for the keyword *Alexa*. As soon as the Echo hears me say *Alexa*, it starts paying attention and recording what I say until I stop talking.

When the Echo thinks I have stopped talking, it sends the complete sentence to Amazon's cloud. The Echo device itself isn't capable of doing very much at all. The smarts are in the cloud.

The Amazon cloud receives my command.

Inside Amazon's cloud, possibly hundreds of computers are put to work figuring out what I said and what I want to have happen. Computers understand what humans say using natural language processing software.

The software parses what I said, and hears *play,* so it knows I want to play something. But what?

Amazon extracts *Etta James* after *play* in the sentence. Amazon now knows I want to play *Etta James.* How does Amazon figure out what I mean by *Etta James?*

A few years ago we uploaded all our old CDs into Amazon's music service. In it, we have a lot of music by Etta; she was an awesome singer.

What Amazon does is search our music library for a match. It looks to see if I have any music by Etta James. And sure enough, it finds that we do. Amazon immediately starts randomly playing a selection of her songs through our Echo.

Result! That's exactly what I wanted to have happen. But what if I didn't have any music by Etta James? Amazon would have kept searching different sources for a match. It would try Pandora, a list of radio stations, it's own music service, and probably a hundred other sources I have no idea about.

Because Amazon could have hundreds of computers working on this one problem in parallel, it can do all this work really fast. Amazon literally searches every possible source of potential Etta James matches at the same time. All the answers are combined and the best answer is selected from the options. That's the power of the cloud. A search on your device could never be as fast or look in as many different places for a match.

Notice we have a little **ecosystem** going on here. Echo is one part of the ecosystem. Our uploaded music is another part of the ecosystem. Over time we have configured Pandora with our preferences. That's part of the ecosystem. All the music we've ever purchased from Amazon is also part of the ecosystem. We have purchased Kindle books with audio narration. That's part of the ecosystem.

We haven't, but other people have configured their Echo to turn lights on and off, to open doors, to change the temperature, and hundreds of other smart home related tricks. That's part of their ecosystem.

We don't, but you can directly call another Echo owner and talk to them over your Echo. It's like a phone call using an Echo device as a phone. If you have an elderly parent and the Echo is how they can call you in an emergency, without having to dial a number, that's a very important part of an ecosystem.

You can start to see how an ecosystem is made up of a system services that build on each other and work together to provide you valuable services. Once we find value in something, we are reluctant to give it up, and that's why we have the *ecosystem wars*.

What do I mean by ecosystem wars?

Every cloud service you use from a cloud provider increases **switching costs**. Say, for example, you are tired of your Echo and would like to switch to Google Home.

This is exactly my situation right now. The problem with Alexa is that she's as dumb as a post. I mean no disrespect. Alexa does a lot of things well, but ask her any kind of difficult question, and the chances are she'll have no idea what you're talking about. It's maddening. Also, Alexa does not learn. Every morning I ask her to play the same radio station and she gets it wrong as often as not.

Google is the leader in AI, so I think Google Home would do

a much better job at answering my questions. The problem is we have tied ourselves to Amazon's ecosystem.

Do I really want to switch bad enough that I'll move all my music to Google? Do I really want to go through the process of Google learning all my preferences? Do I want to forgo having Kindle ebooks read over the Echo?

I honestly don't know. And that's what sucks about ecosystems. From a customer perspective, we want to have it all. We want to pick and choose and have everything just work.

That's not reality, unfortunately. Every major platform wants to create features that are so enticing you'll adopt their ecosystem and never considering moving to another.

That sort of loyalty is worth lots of money, and that's why there's an ecosystem war for your business. Amazon has the early lead, a significant lead, but competition is heating up.

Or I could switch to the Apple ecosystem. I already have an iPhone. I could pay for Apple Music and stream music instead of worrying about preserving old albums. I could take it one step further and get the new LTE watch and stream music over the watch to my new AppleEarPods. That sounds cool. And Apple has their HomePod that I can use to replace my Echo. But I don't think so. Siri is even dumber than Alexa, so that wouldn't be a win.

You can tell competition is fierce by how the ecosystems treat each other. You can buy everything on Amazon, right? Search for Google Home on Amazon. You won't find it. Amazon doesn't allow Google Home to be sold on Amazon.

Until recently the Amazon Prime Video app was not available on Apple TV. It took negotiation between Apple and Amazon to make it happen. Amazon doesn't sell Google's Chromecast and other Google gear, nor does Amazon sell Apple TV devices.

See how this works? These are the kind of decisions Apple, Google, and Amazon want us to make. They want to force us into adopting one ecosystem: *theirs*. We don't get to have it all.

Petty? Childish? Bad for customers? Yes, I think so. But that's how seriously all the players take this ecosystem stuff.

It's war. A war for customers.

In a way picking a service is a lot like getting married. When you get married, you're marrying into a new family. When picking a service, you're marrying into an ecosystem. Pick your in-laws well.

Facebook Memories

Facebook loves to do little things for us in the background.

The goal is to keep us spending more time on Facebook. And it works.

Here's an example of Facebook surfacing a memory of mine from 3 years ago. It's our car just before we were about to set off on a cross-country trip.

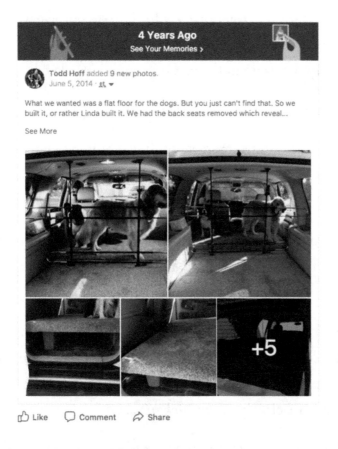

Birthdays are another example of Facebook doing stuff for us in the background. Facebook reminds us of everyone's birthdays and even creates a personal video to share for the occasion.

What does 'in the background' mean?

When something happens in the background, it happens *behind the scenes*. You don't ask for it. Like sausage, you don't see it being made, you don't care how it gets made, but it magically shows up in the grocery store every day.

That's how Facebook Memories works, *in the background*.

Facebook creates Memories for all two billion of its users. Can you imagine all the computers working their CPUs to the bone to do all this for us?

Did anyone ask for Memories? No. Facebook thought we'd like this feature, so they used all their data, cloud computing capacity, and programming talent to make it happen.

Memories is implemented in Facebook's cloud. It runs in Facebook's cloud continuously. Facebook is always generating Memories without anyone making a request. So, its happens proactively *in the background*.

We'll see more and more proactive features as time goes on. Once you have data in the cloud, there's no end of clever features that can made.

Google Photos

Google Photos is Google's service for storing and organizing photos.

All the photos I take on my iPhone upload to Google Photos. Why not use Apple's photo app? Because Google Photos is so much better, largely because it's a cloud service. Google processes all uploaded photos in their cloud. Apple only processes photos locally on each device. Apple has better privacy, but Google has better AI, and it lets you do some incredible things.

Ask Google Photos to see all your pictures of dogs and it will find every picture you have with a dog in it.

Here are the first few pictures of what Google Photos returns when I ask to see all my dog pictures. I have a lot of dog pictures.

How does a computer know what a dog looks like? Through

AI (artificial intelligence). Google has trained software to look at a photo and know when it contains an image of a dog.

That's just the start of what you can do. You can ask to see all pictures containing the color blue, or pictures with clouds, or pictures taken in California, or pictures taken at a certain time or date range, or pictures of an event.

It's amazing. The AI Google uses to search photos is incredibly powerful.

One huge benefit is you don't have to spend hours painstakingly organizing photos anymore (which admit it, you never did anyway). Just search for what you want, and Google will organize the results for you.

That's the power of the cloud, and it will only get better over time as Google's AI improves.

So that's Google Photos the cloud service, what does Photos do for us proactively?

Google Photos likes to use AI to "improve" your pictures.

Here's an example of what Google calls *Stylized* photos. My original photo looks like:

One day Google notified me it thought my picture could look better. Here's what it came up with:

Google applied some tweaks my picture. Does Google's photo better look than mine? I don't think so in this case, but some changes it makes look pretty cool.

The point of the story is that improving photos is something Google does proactively. Somewhere in Google's cloud an AI looks at all your pictures, determines which ones it thinks it can improve, makes those improvements, and proudly shows you its handiwork.

While Stylized photos are cool, much cooler are the *trip Albums* Google automatically puts together.

The extraordinary rains we received in California in 2016 made for an incredible wildflower season. We decided to go on a road trip and take a look. As you might imagine, I took a lot of photos.

Here's an example of an album Google put together of our wildflower trip:

Trip to Joshua Tree and San Luis Obispo County

Apr 19-20

📍 San Luis Obispo County

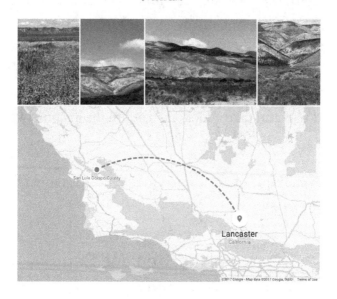

Soda Lake

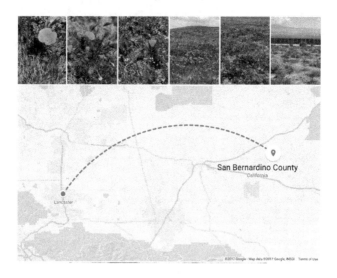

Antelope Valley California Poppy Reserve State Natural Reserve

I did not make this. Google put this album together, automatically, on its own, and shared it with me.

Somewhere in Google's cloud software noticed my photos were close together in time and space, so it figured I must have taken a trip. It probably looks at the pictures and thinks to itself, "yeah, those look pretty good, let's make an album. Todd will really like that."

And Google was right. I loved the album. Mostly I loved not having to make it myself! Albums are so much work to create. I have lots of albums like this that Google has made for me of various trips.

Google makes other things as well. If Google notices photos

were taken close together, it will combine them into an *animation*. I'd show you, but you can't see animations in a book.

Google also has it's own feature, similar to Facebook Memories, that it calls *Rediscover This Day*.

Rediscover this day

The larger point is Google has built an AI that understands video and photos at a deep level. Google uses that knowledge and the power of its cloud to make delightful creations in the background. This has never been done before because it never could be done before. I can't wait to see what they create next.

Google Home

Google Home is Google's version of the Amazon Echo. I showed a picture of it earlier in this chapter.

Like Amazon Echo, Google Home can do a lot of cool stuff:

- OK Google, order an Uber.
- Hey Google, remind me to buy strawberries next time I'm at the Costco in Santa Cruz
- OK Google, reorder Old Spice deodorant.
- Hey Google, How long is my commute?
- Hey Google, make it cooler.
- Hey Google, where is Alaska Flight 21 right now?
- OK Google, call mom.
- Hey Google, add pick Linda up at 6:00 today to my calendar
- OK Google, remember that the house keys are in the bushes

The Echo is still the winner in the shear number of different things it can do. Google's playing from behind, but it's catching up.

What Google hopes is its lead in AI technology will attract users to their ecosystem. How? By Google Home being able to do smarter and more sophisticated things than anyone else.

Here's an example of something Google can do that Amazon can't do: "Hey Google, remind me to buy strawberries next time I'm at the Costco in Santa Cruz."

Let's unpack this. Google Home is a cloud service, so it works like the Echo. Google Home notices I said *Hey Google*. It then passes whatever I say to Google's cloud. Like the Echo, possibly hundreds of computers will work on figuring out what I said, what I meant, and what I want to have happen.

Google will see that I said *remind me*. So it knows I'm creating a reminder. A reminder for what? A reminder *to buy strawberries*. The difference here is Google knows what *strawberries* are. It knows strawberries can be bought in stores and it uses that information to create richer services.

That's why Google can make sense of *next time I'm at the Costco in Santa Cruz*. Like a human Google can reason from my wanting a thing called a strawberry, to knowing what *next time* means, and knowing what *Costco in Santa Cruz* means, to build an alert that will notify me once and only once that I should buy strawberries if I'm in the store.

To make this work, Google has to have a lot of practical knowledge. It has to understand what *next time* means. It has to understand *Costco in Santa Cruz* is a particular physical location. I can't be at just any store, or any Costco, or anywhere in Santa Cruz. I must be in the Costco in Santa Cruz. Nowhere else.

That's powerful stuff. It's not simple at all to implement. In Google's cloud, there's some piece of software that's constantly watching my location and then triggering the notification. When I leave the store it must know to cancel the alert because that's what *next time* means. It gets complicated fast.

And Google is doing this for potentially billions of people, all over the world, all of which may have multiple such reminders outstanding at anyone time.

Now that's *proactive* and *in the background.*

Sophisticated proactive services like these will become the norm as AI gets better, as clouds become more powerful, and ecosystems try even harder to capture you into their orbit.

24

DOES STORMY WEATHER AFFECT CLOUD COMPUTING?

I read a report that said 51% of people think stormy weather affects cloud computing.

Given all we've learned so far, do you think this:

affects cloud computing?

This is a test, so consider carefully...

If you said "no, that's just silly," then great job! You're right.

My guess is 51% of people think cloud computing has something actually to do with the clouds they see in the sky. So they reason "Sure, storms would impact cloud computing, whatever that is."

But we know better. We know the clouds in the sky are not the same clouds in cloud computing.

If you said "Yes, storms can affect cloud computing," then great job! You're right.

Wait, how can both answers be right?

Storms can affect cloud computing, but not in the simple-minded way implied by the survey result.

Severe storms can cause flooding, power outages and networks to fail. Any datacenter assaulted by a brutal storm is at risk. And since the cloud runs inside datacenters, the cloud is also at risk.

But we know properly architected software can survive the failure of a single datacenter. Software can adapt by failing over to another datacenter in the same availability zone or even to a datacenter in a different region.

In that sense, the cloud can't be affected by a storm. The

cloud is bigger than any single datacenter or any single region. The cloud is a gigantic interconnected system spanning the entire globe. The cloud can handle any number of users. The cloud can handle any amount of traffic. The cloud can be programmed to do whatever you want. The cloud can adapt to any failure. That's the true power of the cloud.

This wasn't a trick question, but the answer was tricky.

So how did you do?

The only wrong answer here is thinking clouds in the sky are the same clouds in cloud computing. I've failed you if you're not sure on this point. Please reread the book from the beginning.

If you aced this test, then there's just one more test before our journey together comes to an end.

25

IF I SAY SOMETHING IS IN THE CLOUD, DO YOU KNOW WHAT IT MEANS?

OK, let's just try another little test to see if I delivered on my promise of explaining the cloud.

Tulip is a Dating Service in the Cloud

You're in café, sipping a beverage. From a nearby table, you overhear a snippet of conversation. A young woman says, "I just signed up for Tulip, it's an awesome new cloud dating service."

When you hear something like *Tulip is in the cloud*, you should understand what that means now. It should mean something concrete and real to you. Does it?

I hope it does. Here's what I hope pops into your mind:

- Hey, I know what a cloud service is now because I read that great book by what's his name, you know, *Explain the Cloud Like I'm 10*. Awesome book. I'm so glad I rated it 5 stars on Amazon. Earned some good karma for that.
- I know what a cloud is. A cloud is just a bunch of computers in a datacenter.
- I know what a datacenter is. A datacenter is a giant warehouse-sized building containing lots and lots of computers and other equipment.
- I know what a service is. A service is a job I hire someone to do for me.
- I know what a cloud service is. A cloud service performs a job for me in a cloud.
- What service is being performed for me? Well, Tulip is a dating service, so the service must be related to dating.
- I know I'm going to access Tulip using one of my devices, like my phone, tablet, or on my computer using a web browser.
- I know the cloud is a separate place, it's not on my device; I access the cloud over the internet using an app or web site.
- I know what the internet is. The internet is an electronic highway system for sending data from one computer to another computer.

- I know the thing on a device that knows how to access the cloud is called a *program* or *app*.
- I know that I'll have to download Tulip's app onto my device to use their cloud service. Or, if their service is implemented on the web, I'll have to go to Tulip's website to use the service. Either way, it works the same for me.
- I know I'll use the Tulip app (or website) to perform some job for me, like hook me up with a date. My request to find a date will be sent, as data, over the internet to a computer in Tulip's cloud.
- I know Tulip may have created its own cloud or might have rented cloud services from a cloud provider.
- I know a computer in Tulip's cloud will receive my request to find a date. It will do the work of matching my profile to a list of worthy candidates. It will return the list, over the internet, to Tulip's app. The app will display my matches and let me accept or reject them.
- I know all my dating data is mostly safe in the cloud, but I also know accidents can and do happen. Data can be lost, and security is always something to be mindful of.
- I know I can access Tulip from anywhere there's an internet connection.

- I know Tulip's dating service can handle an infinite number of users, as long as someone pays the bill.
- I know the dating service, because it's in the cloud, has a lot of available compute power to implement powerful features. It can find me the best match possible by searching using machine learning. It can create proactive features like notifying me when a new member might make a good match.
- Hey, I know a lot about the cloud now. Yay!

Now that we're warmed up, let's try another scenario.

Smart Home in the Cloud

Here's a great cloud service example from an episode of the Netflix show *Grace and Frankie*.

A couple in the show just bought an expensive new house. After failing to set the temperature with a fancy thermostat, one character waves his hands in the air and says, "This is a smart house, it's all in the cloud." The second character, looking puzzled, says, "What does that mean?" The first character shrugs and replies, "I don't know."

I laughed out loud! I immediately thought those characters should buy this book! Then they would know what *all in the cloud* means and that they might be able to predict from just that one clue how the entire system works.

We have ourselves a little detective story here, let's explore the clues.

First, let's establish what we know:

- This is a high-end smart house.
- There's a thermostat on the wall the new homeowner has no clue how to use.
- The homeowner knows the temperature for the house is controlled in the cloud, but they aren't sure what that means or how it works.

Let's start deducing.

The very word *smart* in smart house implies the house is controlled by a computer. We just don't know how yet.

We can infer that since the homeowner has not seen this kind of thermostat before, it's not your standard issue thermostat. They would know how to use one of those.

We can infer that since the home is controlled in the cloud that there's a cloud service involved. Some sort of service in the cloud is helping control the house.

We know cloud services are accessed using some sort of device. What's the device in this example? It's not one we've talked about before.

That's right, it's the thermostat. What an unforeseen twist in the plot! The thermostat is the interface through which the house temperature is controlled.

So we know immediately the thermostat is not the dumb kind of thermostat houses usually have, it must be some kind of computer. Only a computer can talk to the cloud.

That brings up another thing we now know. We know to talk to the cloud the thermostat has to be on the internet. That means the thermostat has to be connected to the internet, almost certainly over the home wifi system.

So we know quite a bit already, don't we? With just a few clues we were able to figure out a lot.

There's a lot we still don't know. To figure out more, we'll have to know more about the thermostat.

Which thermostat were they using? I'm not sure. Here's a picture of a possible candidate, the *Nest Learning Thermostat*.

Nest's claim to fame is that it learns over time how you like to heat and cool your house.

You train it by adjusting the temperature. While you're adjusting the temperature Nest learns what you like. It learns what temperature you prefer at night, in the morning, on the weekends, and so on.

Nest obviously has sensors for measuring the temperature, but it also has sensors to detect if anyone is at home or not. If nobody is at home, Nest puts the house in energy saving mode. I did some research and Nest calls this their *activity sensor*. Nest also has a *humidity sensor*.

Let's assume the thermostat in the show was a Nest, or at least something very much like it.

I can understand why the characters in the show were perplexed. If you came upon a Nest thermostat without having any idea what it was or how it worked, you might justifiably be baffled. It's not clear changing the temperature requires spinning the outside ring of the device. It's not clear tapping on the screen brings up an interface for controlling the device. It's not clear Nest can be controlled by an iPhone app. And it's not clear at all it's connected over wifi to the cloud.

But I think knowing it's a smart house we would be able to infer most of the above. We know Nest must be a smart device, so it must have some sort of user interface. We would poke and prod it until it did something.

We would also know to lookup Nest using Google to see how it works. From there, we would learn there was an iPhone app for controlling the device. We would download the app.

After downloading the app, we would learn our Nest can be controlled from anywhere in the world using the app. That has deep implications. It means the iPhone doesn't have to be close to the device to control it. That tells us a lot about how the system works.

The app must talk to the Nest cloud service because it can't talk to the device from far away. Any changes made through the app actually make changes in the cloud service, not directly on the device. Later, the Nest cloud service talks to your Nest, relaying to it whatever changes were made through the app.

One thing to wonder about is where does the learning occur? On the Nest or in the cloud? I wasn't able to find an answer. But we can think of several possibilities.

A device attached to the wall has to be very careful about how much power it uses. Machine learning using AI (artificial intelligence) is complex. It takes a lot of computer power to learn complex patterns.

That the learning takes place in the cloud makes more sense as there's all the computer power you need to learn the temperature schedule, for a house. Yet, how complex can it be to learn how you like your temperature maintained? Maybe it's simple enough to be done on the device? We just don't know.

Another thing to consider is that home network connectivity is often poor. Nest would have to be very careful about how much it relied on the cloud for its smarts. It should be able to work locally, in the house, even if the network is down and it can't talk to the cloud. How happy would you be if you woke up and your house was freezing because your network was down? Not very happy, I'd imagine.

So we can guess there's a close cooperation between Nest and the cloud. My guess is the Nest cloud service takes the lead in the relationship. Since a Nest can be controlled from anywhere in the world, it makes sense the cloud would be in charge of controlling each Nest.

What this means in practice is each Nest is responsible for hitting a target temperature. That's all handled locally, in the house, because the sensors are in the device and the device is smart enough to bring a house to a specified temperature. But it's the cloud service that tells each Nest what to do.

I did some research, but I wasn't able to find the answer. Nest keeps a tight lid on details about how its system works. I think what I'm saying is reasonable though.

During my research, I found Nest is weather aware. That means it adjusts the temperature taking into account weather forecasts.

There are two ways weather forecasts could be integrated—in the cloud or on the device.

Software in the could continuously monitor the weather forecast for each Nest location. Any forecast changes would cause an update to the temperature schedule and those updates would be pushed down to each Nest device.

This is a perfect use of the cloud. There might be a lot of Nest devices, but there are a lot of computers in the cloud. It would be no problem to do this sort of work in the cloud.

Or the work could be performed by each device. Each Nest device is an internet connected computer. Each device could directly contact a weather service, download the weather forecast, and recalculate its own temperature schedule.

Both scenarios are possible. It doesn't really matter for our purposes how it works. These are just some of the issues to consider when thinking about how a cloud-based system works.

How did you do?

The goal was to understand what it means to say *Something is in the cloud*.

Did you have any thoughts like I described when I told you *Tulip is in the cloud*?

How about when I said a *smart house is in the cloud*?

If so, then I did my job and fulfilled my promise.

If I failed you, I'm sorry. Please visit me online at Todd Hoff's Author Page on Facebook. You can ask me questions there. I'll try to make it up to you.

26

WE'VE COME TO THE END OF OUR JOURNEY

I want to thank you for reading my book. I truly appreciate it! More than you can ever know.

If you don't mind, please review this book on amazon.com. It would help me attract more awesome readers like you.

Visit me online at Todd Hoff's Author Page on Facebook. We can chat there.

Want to be notified when I've published something new? Join Todd Hoff's newsletter on MailChimp.

You can also follow me on Todd Hoff's Author Page on Amazon.

And just another reminder, if you have any questions, please feel free to ask me anything on my Facebook page. It would be my pleasure to help.

WHAT READERS ARE SAYING...

They say authors shouldn't read reviews of their books, but I'm so excited to have reviews that I can't help myself. I have ten reviews so far. That's great!

I thank everyone for their reviews. They are the feedback I need to help improve this book. If there any parts I could explain better, I'm more than happy to take another crack at it. If there any subjects you would like me to cover, just let me know.

The reviews let me know I was on target with the tone and level of technical detail. Given how complicated this cloud stuff can be, that's a huge relief.

I was worried about getting too technical. I was also worried that I was so worried about getting too technical that I wouldn't say anything useful.

Hitting the right balance is challenging. I'm happy so far readers are saying I didn't miss the target.

Great book to understand cloud technology. It is really useful to understand how cloud works. And this book will help you with that. For me as software engineer chapter about how Netflix works is the best.

This should be your first cloud book. I selected this book to get a strong foundation in what "being in the cloud" means. I learned that and much more. I am an older backend developer and wanted to start learning about the devops phenomenon. I selected this book in order to learn and appreciate some basic and fundamental concepts first. I highly recommend this book.

Easy Read & Informative. I'm glad I read this book. I'm already a knowledgeable computer user but I still learned some interesting things. Specifically, the origin of the "cloud" and "internet" terms. :)

Five Stars. Very easy and clear reading. The title is actual and honest.

Funny and informative. This is a fun and easy to read book that explains the Cloud in a simple and easy to consume way. Love it!

B2B Cold Cold Callers MUST READ. Yeah, you know who you are. You get the client's script full of technobabble, and your eyes glaze over. If your contract is paying enough to give a cra... ahem... an hour of your time, this book breaks down what the freak these idiots are saying when they go on about the cloud. It's very basic, but gives you the basis to figure out what things like "IaaS" or "develop applications on the cloud" mean.

My response: This review made me realize I didn't explicitly cover IaaS, so I've added a new chapter—What is Cloud Computing?— that explains IaaS in detail. Thanks for the suggestion.

I think is a great book for those who have no idea what the cloud is. It is easy to understand and uses lots of analogies that people can relate to. Obviously there are a million different ideas associated with the cloud but for folks that just want to know what the heck everyone means when the talk about the cloud, this book will help.

An easy read. I am glad I read this book. Truly worth the time. Waiting for such a book on Machine learning and AI ;)

If you don't mind, please review this book on amazon.com. It would help me attract more awesome readers like you!

ALSO BY TODD HOFF

I have a few other books you might also enjoy reading.

The Strange Trial of Ciri: The First Sentient AI

SciFaiku Poetry

The Sacrifice Games

A Very Special Frankenstein Birthday

Your Designer Diet: How to Stay on a Diet for the Rest of Your Life